DISASTER RELIEF

100 Devotions For The Hot Mess

By Laura Cowan

Spilt Cup Publishing

Spilt Cup
PUBLISHING
www.spiltcup.com

© 2023 Laura Cowan

All rights reserved. No portion of this book may be reproduced, stored in any retrieval system, or transmitted in any form or by any means without express written consent.

Unless otherwise indicated, all Scripture quotations are taken from the Holy Bible, New Living Translation, copyright © 1996, 2004, 2015 by Tyndale House Foundation. Used by permission of Tyndale House Publishers, Carol Stream, Illinois 60188. All rights reserved.

Scripture quotations marked (NKJV) are taken from the New King James Version®. Copyright © 1982 by Thomas Nelson. Used by permission. All rights reserved.

Scripture quotations marked (NET) are from the NET Bible® copyright ©1996, 2019 by Biblical Studies Press, L.L.C. http://netbible.com All rights reserved

Scripture quotations marked (NIV) are taken from the Holy Bible, New International Version®, NIV®. Copyright © 1973, 1978, 1984, 2011 by Biblica, Inc.® Used by permission of Zondervan. All rights reserved worldwide. www.zondervan.com The "NIV" and "New International Version" are trademarks registered in the United States Patent and Trademark Office by Biblica, Inc.®

Scripture quotations marked (NASB®) are taken from the New American Standard Bible®, Copyright © 1995 by The Lockman Foundation. Used by permission. All rights reserved. lockman.org

Scripture quotations marked (MSG) are taken from The Message, copyright © 1993, 2002, 2018 by Eugene H. Peterson. Used by permission of NavPress. All rights reserved. Represented by Tyndale House Publishers.

Scripture quotations marked (CEV) are from the Contemporary English Version Copyright © 1991, 1992, 1995 by American Bible Society. Used by Permission.

Scripture quotations marked (ESV) are from the ESV® Bible (The Holy Bible, English Standard Version®), © 2001 by Crossway, a publishing ministry of Good News Publishers. Used by permission. All rights reserved. The ESV text may not be quoted in any publication made available to the public by a Creative Commons license. The ESV may not be translated in whole or in part into any other language.

Scripture quotations marked (AMP) are taken from the Amplified® Bible, Copyright © 2015 by The Lockman Foundation. Used by permission. lockman.org

Scripture quotations marked (Darby) are taken from the DARBY BIBLE, published in 1867, 1872, 1884, 1890; public domain.

Translational emendations, amplifications, and paraphrases are by the author.

ISBN: 9798860823501
Imprint: Spilt Cup Publishing

DEDICATION

Thank you to all who buy this book. Without you,
our electricity could be shut off.

To "My Favorite Everything," John, who's loved me so well
these fifty-plus years, and likes my cooking.

To my eight children who raised me.
Now put that down before you poke your eye out.

To my grandkids, because—GRANDKIDS!

To my six siblings—my first friends;
always there to rely on— and tell on.

To all related to me whether by blood or marriage or church.
I'll never intentionally send you to voicemail. You're that
important to me. But would you please consider getting the
Marco Polo app?

And ALL praise and thanks to my Wonderful Counselor,
Almighty God, Who turns my stale crusts and carp bones
into loaves and fishes for His glory.

INTRODUCTION

My day started well: good coffee, all the comforts of a quiet morning—Bible, journal, favorite pen…and then I tripped, baptizing everything in hot java. The longer I stared at the mess, the more it reminded me of something: Oh yeah—my life.

But I recalled the adage, "When life gives you lemons, make Poo-Pourri," so I snapped a picture, knowing someday I'd reflect on it and say, "Who took this and why?"

Well, it's now the cover photo of this book as a tiny reminder that God uses the mess, stress, and permanent press of life to work good things in us.

A note about the verses connected to these devotions: Back in the day, I viewed the Bible like, "My friend wrote a book, so I guess I'd better read it (sigh)." I've since learned that God's Word is the singular source of strength to endure the manure of life.

The goal of *my* book is to highlight *His* Book.

A secondary goal is to encourage you regarding morning devotions: Get a travel mug with a tight-fitting lid.

1

Take This Cup

Hello, my name is Laura Cowan, and I'm a recovering aqua-phobe. I'm not really afraid of water; I just come from a long line of women who don't drink water. My mother and grandmother—bless their dehydrated little hearts—credit their longevity to lukewarm coffee: one cup, sipped all day. The sins of my parents have been passed to me. The mere thought of guzzling a half-gallon of water each day is enough to drive me to drink…just not water.

But as I said, I'm recovering. I bought two eight-ounce glasses from the thrift store; placed one in the bathroom and one in the kitchen. I keep them filled, and every time I go into either room, I drink that little cup and refill it so it's ready for the next time around. Now my kidneys gush with gratitude, and my UTIs are MIA.

This principle of little sips has helped me in every arena of life. Parenting is absolutely daunting. Eighteen years without parole is enough to scare anyone unless we take it one nose-wipe, hug, and instructive lesson at a time. And repentance— the turning away from things that undermine life in Christ— is like U.S. Route 20, the longest road in America, unless we view progress one swallow at a time. You confessed? You're halfway home. You asked for help? The destination is in view.

And so it is with a life of faith. We get up, seek the Lord, and do the thing right in front of us. We drink from the cup of salvation, one sip at a time.

I will lift up the cup of salvation and praise
the LORD's name for saving me.
Psalm 116:13

Give us today our needed bread.
Matt. 6:11 (Darby)

2

THE SECRET TO WISDOM

I've discovered the secret to wisdom: Think of something an idiot would say, then don't say it.

There may be more to wisdom, but given a mouth like mine, this is a good place to start. At least I'd avoid tactless comments like, "Oh. My. GOSH. The fast-food workers here exude the enthusiasm of limp fries," and then discover I'm speaking to one. I mean a worker, not a limp fry . . . though she sure . . . well—you get my point.

Mother Theresa said, "Words that do not give the Light of Christ increase the darkness."

My mouth can be an absolute black hole of disparaging remarks, and there's only one solution; Psalm 141:3: "Set a guard, oh Lord, over my mouth; keep watch over the door of my lips . . ." use duct tape if necessary (I added the last bit because it works, and I'm just that desperate).

But silence is only the first step. I want to speak apt words, fitting words; "The word that sustains the weary" (Isaiah 50:4).

For that, my mind needs the Holy Spirit on continuous feed.

There's plenty of darkness to go around. To speak the Light that dispels darkness— that's the goal, and perhaps, the true secret to wisdom.

When she speaks, her words are wise and
she gives instruction with kindness.
Proverbs 31:26

A wise woman builds her home, but a foolish
woman tears it down with her own hands.
Proverbs 14:1

Death and life are in the power of the tongue.
Proverbs 18:21

3

IF THE SHOE FITS

In the story of Cinderella, the wicked step-sister coerces and crushes her super-sized foot into the glass slipper, striving to win the prince—that guy in baby-blue designer tights. No accounting for some people's taste.

But I can relate to the striving. Sometimes I want something so badly I attempt to force my square-peg craving into the round hole of God's will. I go at it from every angle; bargaining, justifying, promising to glorify Him with this shiny trinket if He'll just gimme— pleeeeze… Ignoring the voice whispering, "Laura, this just isn't a good fit for you…"

Sometimes through sheer determination, I manage to make the shoe fit. "Yes, I see that…" the Lord says, "…But can you *walk* in it." He waits, arms folded, watching my spiritual gymnastics, knowing eventually I'll hobble over to Him with, "Um…Lord, can you help me get this OFF?"

He exchanges it for one custom-fit, flexible, with firm support and a soft-in-her-soul quality.

If the shoe fits, wear it. But life's too short, and the road's too hard for walking in anything other than His will.

I have the bunions to prove it.

And your ears shall hear a word behind you saying, 'This is the way, walk in it.
Isaiah 30:21 ESV

If you follow me, you won't have to walk in darkness, because you will have the light that leads to life.
John 8:12

4

Marching Orders

I'm going to stay home. No. I'd better go into the church. No. I need to work on my project. Or maybe not work on my project but finish the laundry. Or get that email sent off and go to tothestoreorseewhatyouguysonfacebookareup tolthinkIdranktoomuchcoffeeandaaaaaccccckkk!

It's one of those mornings.

"Among those nations you will find no peace or rest (Deut. 28:65). "Those nations" being all the flurry and worry in me. I need my "government to be upon His shoulders," and to take my cues from King David, who, when harassed by life, said, "I'm taking to my bed." Oh wait—that was me. David said, "Oh God, we meditate on Your unfailing love…"

So I think I'll just sit here a minute and breathe.
Inhale: "Be still and know that I am God" (Psalm 46:10).
Exhale: "Give all your worries and cares to God because He cares for you" (1 Peter 5:7).
Inhale: "Come to me, you who are weary and heavy-burdened, and I will give you rest" (Matthew 11:28).
Exhale: "In quietness and confidence is your strength…"
Inhale: "But you would have none of it" (Isaiah 30:15).
Until now: *Exhale*.

What should I do when I don't know what to do? The Message Bible refreshes a familiar passage from Proverbs 3:5,6: "Trust the Lord from the bottom of your heart; don't try to figure things out on your own. Listen for God's voice in everything you do, everywhere you go; He's the One who will keep you on track."

It's time to head out to Women's Bible Study.

"March on with courage, my soul" (Judges 5:21).

5

FAITH TO FAITH

I took a poll of all my thoughts, and the vote was unanimous: John was the cutest, smartest, kindest guy in college. We had four classes together, including a trampoline class, so by the time we started dating, I was well acquainted with the virtues of his legs. Wait—did I just say legs? I meant character, the virtues of his character.

Through him, I gave my life to Jesus Christ. Soon after, we married. For the first few years, my Christian walk was so entwined with John's, that my faith in Jesus was, to a great extent, faith in John.

A near-death experience via a gunman and the ensuing threat to our lives forced me to examine my personal relationship with Jesus and question my faith: Maybe my connection to Christ is solely through osmosis. Is it possible "this little light of mine" is merely the broad glow of John's steadfast faith? What does trust look like? Who is my lifeline to God—John or Jesus? If John was taken from me, would I trust the Lord, or would fear be Lord of my life? I had to choose.

The decision to trust occurs in a moment, but learning to trust occurs over a lifetime of such moments, reinforced by daily choices:

- To obey His Word rather than my impulses.
- To rely on His ability in the face of impossibility.
- To know even if the worst of my fears are realized, He will be there in that most dreaded place.

And—perhaps the most challenging:

- To cry out to Him when I have miserably, thoroughly, and continuously failed all of the above.

My faith is solely my own, and wholly in Christ.

*You cried to me in trouble, and I saved you;
I answered out of the thundercloud and tested
your faith when there was no water...*
Psalm 81:7

*Examine yourselves to see if your faith
is genuine. Test yourselves.*
2 Corinthians 13:5

6

OUT OF THE ASHES

My brother-in-law owns property within Yosemite National Park. A few years ago, a raging fire burned acres upon acres of forest, coming within mere feet of their newly-built home. When the ashes cooled, the devastation unveiled a remarkable sight formerly hidden by brush and trees: A glorious view of El Capitan, Half-Dome, and Cloud's Rest. Those granite fortresses had always existed, but it took a fire to reveal their presence.

The prophet Isaiah experienced such a fire. The benefits and comforts of being a companion to the king went up in smoke with the death of King Uzziah. Isaiah begins this new chapter of his life with this: "In the year that King Uzziah died I saw the Lord sitting upon a throne..." (Isaiah 6:1 ESV).

Isaiah describes all he sees from this new perspective, born out of grief and loss. What follows is a new Isaiah, a new ministry, and a new relationship with the Lord.

Likewise, in my life, a consuming fire— a burning away of attachments, the familiar, and even what is "safe" is often necessary for me to see Jesus Christ for who He really is rather than what I've heard or imagined Him to be.

I fear the process, forgetting His intent is not to destroy me but to destroy the things obstructing my view of Him and His plan for me.

From the ash of "All is Lost!" rises "All is Gained!" when my eyes see clearly El Capitan, My Captain, My Christ.

I have lost all things…that I may
gain Christ…to know Him…
(Read Philippians 3:7-11)

To all who mourn…he will give a crown of beauty for ashes, a joyous blessing instead of mourning, festive praise instead of despair…
Isaiah 61:3

7

All-Purpose Cleaner

It's a ticking bomb found in public places, randomly detonating with the roar of a lion.

I'm talking about automatic flush toilets. They mean well, but do we really need our backsides sprayed with an international smorgasbord of bacteria? (Note: Do NOT google "germs and automatic flush toilets" unless your gag reflex is non-operational.)

I suggest for efficiency sake, installing a wide selection of automatic dispensers marked "E-coli, Streptococcus, Hepatitis A and Who-Knows-What-All," that we might contaminate as per individual preferences.

Enter wipes. Wipes of every kind: Diaper wipes, facial wipes, hand wipes, disinfectant wipes, personal wipes, scented, unscented, hypoallergenic, MI-free, paraben-free, and alcohol-free; with aloe, vitamin E—and get this: green tea— I'm guessing for those times when sucking on a wipe just seems the right thing to do. Then there are organic wipes, flushable, quilted for extra comfort, triple-layered, and one that boasts of our evolutionary progress: "Made with 99% water!"

But in case you drop your phone in the toilet as you leap before the detonator blows, I suggest you forget about wipes and just use your shirt.

Like unseen bacteria, spiritual contaminants continually mist us—sometimes jetting us—and, like a lion, seek to devour: Pop-up porn, enticing ads, and Facebook rants. As if that weren't enough, we have the deadly schemes of our own secret, hateful, and desperate little thoughts, encouraged and goaded by the devil himself.

Thankfully we have a better—than—wipe, all-purpose cleansing solution: God's Word, the Bible. That humble, no—frills, dusty little book on the shelf reaches into hidden areas of our souls, providing cleansing and refreshing. It's a hot shower in a handy carrying case.

Simply open, read the instructions, and apply daily.

Some of you were like that. But you were cleansed;
you were made holy; you were made right with God
by calling on the name of the Lord Jesus Christ
and by the Spirit of our God.
1 Corinthians 6:11

Christ loved the church and gave himself
up for her to make her holy and clean, washed by
the cleansing of God's word.
Ephesians 5:25,26

I will sprinkle clean water on you, and you will
be clean. Your filth will be washed away, and you will no
longer worship idols. And I will give you
a new heart, and I will put a new spirit in you.
Ezekiel 36:25,26,

8

DEATH BY MINTS

I fasted before the lab tests, just in case they'd forgotten to tell me. This wasn't my first rodeo. I was feeling pretty smug as I followed the technician down the hall as she studied my lab sheet.

"So—let's see… when was the last time you ate?"

"12 hours ago."

"Great….and no coffee, or gum or mints or…" She continued.

"Nope, no coffee, gum…oh…well…uh…I did have three little Altoids just a few minutes ago…"

She came to such an abrupt halt I nearly ran into the back of her. You'd think I'd said, "Two all-beef patties, special sauce, lettuce, cheese, pickles, onions on a sesame seed bun."

Well, one thing led to another, and 20 hours later, I ended up the poster child for World Hunger—well, in my shallow little world, anyway.

Sucking three mini-mints isn't exactly an indulgence. What effect could they have on the big picture? I should've messed up on an accidental hot-fudge sundae.

Turns out, those nonpareils are a real peril to lab tests. They distort the truth and, thus, the outcome of the tests, assessments, and treatments.

All this got me thinking about other indulgences I consider harmless— like moodiness, worry, and self-pity. Mini-sins— or so I rationalize. But they, too, distort truth and, if not acknowledged, affect my overall responsiveness to the Lord and others. Better to confess it and start over.

I don't want to end up the poster child for Soul Hunger.

> Catch all the foxes, those little foxes,
> before they ruin the vineyard of love…
> Song of Songs 2:15

> A wise person is hungry for knowledge,
> while the fool feeds on trash.
> Proverbs 15:14

9
SMELL THAT?

It greeted us at the door after our long trip. It was there, then it wasn't, then it was. A funny odor. Like dead-raccoon-in-the-wall funny. I sniffed in all the obvious places: the kitchen trash, the hamper... I even gave John a hug— sniff-sniff. He backed away.

"Laura, what are you doing?"

"Don't you SMELL that?!" I said.

He gave one token sniff, "Nope."

An hour later, I pulled out a refrigerator drawer: A petrified carrot, an apple-head doll, and...OH DISGUSTING!!! Who knew an innocent spud could become a root of mass destruction, emitting enough methane to solve the gas crisis? I wrapped it in newspaper burial clothes and disposed of it. Apparently, the poor thing had a bout of diarrhea before it died, so I disinfected the drawer, too. Mission accomplished.

But that very same week, I experienced this again in the spiritual realm. Something was off—sort of...yeah...no; no... YES. John was...clearly...well... kind of aloof, or silent— malfunctioning—which isn't like him. Communication was stretched tight and scrambled, like yarn the cat got hold of. I sniffed around but couldn't find the source of the trouble, so I gave up and prayed, "Lord, what is this?"

You're not going to believe it. The answer was me. I was malfunctioning. So focused on an imaginary fingerling in John's eye, I couldn't see the russet in my own. I was harp-y, bossy, and critical.

After apologizing to John for being…well—me, and praying together, we're back to functioning as the happiest couple in the history of marriage, because when we ask the Lord for help, He doesn't leave us rotting in our own juices. He'll expose our sin, not merely to reveal, but to heal— and purify us like Yukon Gold.

Examine me, and probe my thoughts!
Test me, and know my concerns!
Psalm 139:23 NET

And see if there be any hurtful way in me,
and lead me in the everlasting way.
Psalm 139:24 NASB95

Finally, I confessed all my sins to you and
stopped trying to hide my guilt. I said to myself,
"I will confess my rebellion to the LORD."
And you forgave me! All my guilt is gone.
Psalm 32:5

10

Dead-man's Float

I nearly drowned in the Feather River when I was six years old. The sandy bottom was firm under my feet, and then… it wasn't. My dad, seeing a blonde muskrat floating down the river, realized it was my head and yanked me out. He decided that day to teach me the dead-man's float.

Despite his strong arms holding me, I clung, cried, and flailed until exhaustion overrode my terror. When I stopped fighting the water, I could float. Eventually, I learned not only to survive but swim; to breathe, cut a path through the water, to enjoy the rhythm and the freedom that feels like flying.

Many years later, my husband John and I witnessed a murder. The gunman was connected to a mafia group, and a hitman was assigned to kill John. Terra firma disappeared. I could not touch bottom and sank into mirky depths of depression. I clung and cried to the Lord, "Where were You? Where are you now?"

He answered by teaching me the dead-man's float. He taught me to stop fighting life's uncontrollable currents, to release and relax into an unseen hope, to trust His hands holding me, catching me, lifting me up for air.

I not only survived, I learned to live. I discovered Jesus was there, Jesus is here: "The eternal God is your dwelling place, and underneath are the everlasting arms" (Deuteronomy 33:27 ESV).

If we stop flailing long enough to hear His voice and surrender, we'll do more than survive. We'll overcome fear — a freedom that feels like flying.

> When you pass through the waters, I will be with you; When you pass through the rivers, they will not sweep over you.
> Isaiah 43:2

> I sank beneath the waves, and the waters closed over me. Seaweed wrapped itself around my head… But you, O LORD my God, snatched me from the jaws of death!
> Jonah 2:5, 6

> Be still, and know that I am God!
> Psalm 37:7

11

HELP WANTED

I learned five truths as a young Catholic girl. The first two were:

1. God is real.
2. So is the Devil.

The other three were:

"A lawyer, a rabbi, and a priest walk into a bar…"

Don't blame the nuns. They tried. I was probably high from inhaling Holy Day incense.

I did manage to memorize prayers for every occasion. The Hail Mary, for instance, which, contrary to the beliefs of some of my sports-minded friends, has nothing to do with football. But to my child-mind at the time, it had something to do with underwear: "…and blessed is the Fruit of the Loom, Jesus." Or it did, until I was corrected…"Ohhhhh, it's 'fruit of Thy *womb*, Jesus.'" I didn't even know Jesus had a womb.

Then at age seven, I learned "The Act of Contrition," which begins, "OMG, I am hardly sorry for having offended Thee." The phrase is actually, "I am HEARTILY sorry." An excellent prayer. Still, my version more aptly describes my wicked little heart at that age.

Now, as an adult, I've "put away childish things," but I do have a time-worn liturgical prayer available to both Catholics and non-Catholics alike, and I use it frequently.

Though we shouldn't rely on rote religious recitations (Matthew 6:7), God always answers this prayer. It goes like this: "Almighty God... Help, help, helphelphelphelp..."

This word is used 225 times (though not all at once) in 216 verses in the New International Bible, less in the King James Version (perhaps the New International Version needs more help).

God does not weary of our asking. He wearies of our *not* asking. The Psalmist often asks for God's help:

"Listen to my cry for help" (Psalm 5:2).

"Help, O LORD" (Psalm 12:1).

"I prayed to my God for help" (Psalm 17:1).

"Answer our cry for help" (Psalm 20:9).

"I groan for help" (Psalm 22:1).

"Hear my cry, O Lord," is a repeated prayer in Psalms, and while it helps to cry, better to cry for help.

What niggles in your mind right now? Ask for His help, and then *let* Him help.

Helplessness comes from prayerlessness. God's waiting for a sign from you—A HELP WANTED sign.

---✣---

In panic I cried out, 'I am cut off from the LORD!'
But you heard my cry for mercy and
answered my call for help.

Psalm 31:22

My help comes from the Lord,
Maker of heaven and earth.

Psalm 121:2

12

IMPERFECT VERB

Kneeling on the kitchen chair and bent low over the table, our young son Johnny labored intently, designing a cloth banner for Valentine's Day. As he practiced his newly acquired writing skills, his tongue directed every move of the crayon clenched in his fist.

Later, grinning with pride, he held up his finished work. In bold block lettering, the banner read:

"Gob is love."

That he goofed on the lettering did not make God's love any less true. Nor did it in any way detract from Johnny's heart's intent. In fact, his feeble attempt was all the more endearing.

Likewise, our deficient endeavors to love God are cherished by Him. God does not require perfect love. He alone IS perfect love, and He thoroughly delights in our demonstrations to love Him back, as backward as those attempts may be.

Gob is Love.

He has pity on the weak and the needy, and saves them.
Psalm 72:13

A bent reed He will not break off, and a dimly
burning wick He will not extinguish, until
He leads justice to victory.
Matthew 20:12 NASB

13

Breakfast of Champions

I find the cereal aisle disturbing. Over-choice overwhelms. Just give me rolled oats, which are beneath the quick oats, the instant oats in cups or packets, and the new warm and crunchy granola.

We are blessed with abundance, but abundance distracts, confuses, and causes my brain to come to a screeching halt.

As a mom to eight kids, I felt overwhelmed with parenting decisions. How can I lead them when I am not all-knowing, can't read the future, and—let's face it—can't even pick out breakfast cereal?

One morning I looked around as if for the first time and thought, "All these kids- what am I supposed to DO with them??!!" I felt like that little servant girl in the old movie, *Gone With the Wind*: "Mz Scahlet, I dunno nuttin' 'bout birthin' no babies!"

While in that state of panic, this came to mind: Jesus is the Good Shepherd. He does not expect His sheep to know the location of the best grass, the freshest water, the safest pasture—that is His job. The sheep's job is to stay close to Him, stop when He stops, walk when He walks, and trust Him when He says, "Not that way…." No matter what decisions you face today, if He is your shepherd, this is for you: "He shall feed His flock like a shepherd; He shall gather the lambs in His arms, and carry them in His bosom, and shall gently lead those that are with young" (Isaiah 40:11).

I have wandered away like a lost sheep;
come and find me…
Psalm 119:176

My sheep listen to my voice;
I know them, and they follow Me.
John 10:27

14

A Sparrow And A Swallow

During pregnancies, I collected Bible verses to comfort me during the most intense part of the birth process, namely *transition*—cited in medical journals as, "The stage of labor defined by intense contractions, rapid breathing, and screams of 'YOU DID THIS!' to the husband innocently shoveling hospital jello into his mouth."

In this phase, when my eyes began rolling back in my head like a scared horse, John would envelop my face in both hands so that our eyes met and held. Then, phrase-by-phrase, he'd recite a few words of a chosen verse which I'd repeat back to him (along with "groanings too deep for words"), visualizing what was said. A favorite was, "Even the sparrow has found a home, and the swallow a nest for herself, where she may have her young— a place near Your altar, LORD Almighty, my King and my God" (Psalm 84:3).

I was that sparrow; frightened and frail, and I was the swallow; flitting and darting but slowing now… resting… breathing…laying all that is me and my soon-to-be-born in the hands of God.

Today, we labor under the intense pressures of life, the pangs of uncertainty; our thoughts flit and dart from this concern to that sleep-depriving anxiety, and another favored verse from my season of births comes to mind, "Surely I have composed and quieted my heart like a weaned child rests against its mother, my soul is like a weaned child within me" (Psalm 131:2).

Surely I have composed and quieted my heart. This is a discipline, an act of will; I choose to calm my anxious thoughts, to stop the crazy, to "be still and know that He is God" (Psalm 46:10). I feather my nest with reminders of all He created, all He has done in former times, all the times I was sure "The sky is falling!" Yet, it held.

Like a weaned child rests against its mother. A nursing baby is a bicycle-peddling, milk-guzzling bundle of nerves, seeking, snuffling, unable to rest. Only after being filled can she or he snuggle, satisfied, safe, and at ease.

I, too, must drink fully of Jesus Christ and take all He provides, "for he has given us all we need for life and godliness" (2 Peter 1:3).

As Psalm 84:3 reminds me, I have found my home, a nest for myself, where I can lay all my twittering, mouth-gaping neediness at the altar of the Lord, my King, my God.

So, *this* sparrow will swallow, and swallow and swallow, drinking in His promises, His goodness, His Word, and His presence. Until at rest, I reach up and touch His face.

When my anxious thoughts multiply within me,
Your consolations delight my soul.
Psalm 94:19

…He will gently lead the mother sheep
with their young.
Isaiah 40:11

15

Tannin' My Hide

The first time I made acorn bread, I took one bite and spit it out. If this was the standard kitchen fare of California Native tribes, no wonder they hunted elsewhere for grasshoppers, from which perhaps the famed IHOP derives its name.

Acorns contain tannin —enough to tan the hide of a buffalo (the word "tannin" is a derivative of "tanner" and was used for such). I eventually learned—thanks to the Maidu tribe—how to remove the bitter component by peeling, then chopping the acorns, placing them in cheesecloth attached to the bathtub faucet, and letting the water trickle through for a few days to leach out the tannin. What remained was a delicious-tasting nut meat, comparable to hazelnut. It makes a delicious nut bread.

I'm reminded of a similar process needed when someone delivers a bitter accusation. My first reaction is to spit it out. But what if I allowed time, prayer, and the Holy Spirit to "leach out" any irrelevant words yet retain kernels of truth? I'm sure I'd find a morsel to sink my teeth into (even if the deliverer is a nut).

Criticism tests my desire for truth. If ninety percent of an accusation is "tannin," am I willing, for truth's sake, to consider and act upon the other ten percent or even .0005 percent?

I have nothing to defend, and no right to withhold mercy. Romans 2:4 says God's kindness leads us to repentance. How can I *not* pass that kindness on to another? A simple and sincere, "I am so sorry I was not what you needed," can bring healing and a change of heart—both mine and theirs. Then maybe we can go grab a bite together at IHOP.

No one does good, not a single one.
Romans 3:12

Search me, O God, and know my heart...
Point out anything in me that offends you...
Psalm 139:23,24

16
CHECK THE CLOCK

The wall clock in our short-term rental can be seen from the kitchen, dining, and living room. I love its easy-to-read, large block numbers, and pleasant chime. It's everything I want in a clock—except for one thing: it doesn't keep accurate time. It ticks away at a steady pace (I can hear it now from where I sit) but lags behind to varying degrees; it's not even consistently inconsistent. I've tried nursing it along: replacing the batteries, fiddling with gears, and adjusting the hands every morning. I know it's unreliable, but I keep consulting that clock by habit.

Last night, I glanced up from my baking, relieved to see I had another hour before heading off to Bible study. Five minutes later, John stood with his hand on the door, eyeing the myriad of pans, bowls, and batter, and asked,

"Umm...are you about ready? It's five-thirty."

"Five-thirty??!! I thought it was four-twenty!"

With a flurry of flour and apron ties, I scrambled out the door. On my way out, I said nothing to the clock, but I think it sensed my disapproval. I've avoided eye contact all day; I don't have time for this.

The Bible has much to say about reliability: "Putting confidence in an unreliable person... is like chewing with a broken tooth, or walking on a lame foot" (Proverbs 25:19).

"Many claim loyalty, but who is truly reliable" (Proverbs 20:6)?

"Let your 'yes' be yes, and your 'no' be no" (Matthew 5:37).

There are many examples of reliable people and their consequential promotions— Daniel, Joseph, Ruth, and Rahab the prostitute. Others, due to being unreliable, were removed from ministry: King Saul (lied), Ahimaaz (was zealous, but not helpful), Mark (bailed, but repented and was reinstalled) and Demas, who deserted Paul. So I took inventory: Am I truthful, trustworthy, and reliable? Can I be counted on to show up *on time,* and do what I'll do? There's no such thing as being "inconsistently reliable," though "consistently *un*reliable" IS a thing.

If I'm being side-lined in friendship, work, or areas of ministry, maybe it's time to check my clock— before I tic someone off.

If you are untrustworthy about worldly things, who will trust you with the true riches of heaven?
Luke 16:11

Her husband can trust her, and she will
greatly enrich his life.
Proverbs 31:11

[They] must show themselves to be entirely
trustworthy and good. Then they will make the teaching
about God our Savior attractive in every way.
Titus 2:10

17

Heavy Weight Champion

My wrists were not made to carry six bags full of a month's worth of groceries ("a month" is what I tell myself each week as I'm paying for them). My determination to carry it all is some kind of pride thing, like I'm shouting to the world, "I am not as old as I look, and I'll prove it by—OWWWW!"

If John's home when I come dragging in like the Hunchback of Notre Dame, he quickly comes to my rescue, scoops up the load with, "Laura, I've told you to call as you're headed home; I'll do this for you."

Sometimes I struggle with equally heavy bags of anxiety, exhaustion, frustration, fear, and worry. When I recognize this, I take inventory: What am I lugging that Jesus has not asked me to carry? In Matthew 11:30, Jesus says His yoke is easy, and His burden is light. If this is neither easy nor light, what task, responsibility, care, or emotional weight have I taken upon myself?

There is always enough strength, resources, and ability to do God's will, God's way. The unbearable load comes when I attempt my will, my way, or the more disguised version: God's will, my way.

Relationship with Jesus Christ is the first Great Rest. Rest from: "Be your best self." "Do more." "Get all the laundry done," i.e., "manifest the goddess within." I'm pretty sure being my own god is a terrible idea; I manifest plenty of trouble just being my own human. The Great I AM, I am not. He is the Perfect, the Able. As we yoke ourselves to Him, He will manifest His power in us by the Holy Spirit. We are to ask for it and count on it.

The second "rest," once we've come to Christ, is to *continuously* come to Him. He says, "I've told you to call me, I'll handle this."

That's a load off.

… Only in returning to me and resting in me will you be saved. In quietness and confidence is your strength. But you would have none of it.
Isaiah 30:15

Blessed be the Lord, who daily bears our burden, the God who is our salvation.
Psalm 68:19 NASB

Then Jesus said, "Come to me, all you who are weary and carry heavy burdens, and I will give you rest. Take my yoke upon you. Let me teach you, because I am humble and gentle at heart, and you will find rest for your souls. For my yoke is easy to bear and the burden I give you is light.
Matthew 11:28,29

18

A Word For the Bird

Sitting in the morning sun, our cat waited for breakfast, busying herself with the daily grooming ritual: lick paw, rub face, repeat. Suddenly, she froze mid-lick as into her peripheral vision flew a plump little robin, landing on the grass. The cat's tail twitched once, muscles tensed as she lowered herself one millimeter at a time into a full crouch and waited, hidden by flowers. The lone bird peered, head cocked at the ground, distracted by the tantalizing wiggle of a worm. A flash of furry haunches catapulted into the air. I yelled, "HEY!" a split-second before breakfast was served. And now the cat refuses to speak to me.

I'm reminded of 1st Peter 5:8: "Be sober-minded; be watchful. Your adversary the devil prowls around like a roaring lion, seeking someone to devour."

To be sober-minded means to guard your passions. Pay attention. Watch yourself. Monitor your thoughts. Because doing what comes naturally leads to death by natural causes.

Satan is an opportunist; he bides his time, assessing our boundaries, seeking hidden access, or entries left unguarded. He slips in and waits for the lone bird, the distracted bird, the inattentive, happy little fat one, then strikes. His aim is to rob robin, then kill and destroy.

I don't want to be the lone bird or the busy-busy early bird, so focused on getting the worm that I ignore the early cat. I will stay with those who give raucous clamor at the sight of danger and I'll do the same for others, though we may find ourselves on the receiving end of, "Stop that annoying squawking, can't you see I'm…"

And a lone feather descends.

Stay alert. Stay together. Stay alive.

So be on your guard, not asleep like others.
Stay alert and be clearheaded.
1Thessalonians 5:6

You must warn each other every day, while it is still "today," so that none of you will be deceived by sin and hardened against God.
Hebrews 3:13

"Where have you come from?" The LORD asked Satan. Satan answered the LORD, "I have been patrolling the earth, watching everything that's been going on."
Job 1:7

19

What We'll Be, Will Be

I am shocked by the detestable images that pop up on my computer screen, uninvited. I'm talking about my face. I mistakenly hit the FaceTime button. OhMyGOSH! I certainly don't look my age because I'm pretty sure I'd remember turning one hundred twenty-five. Something must be done about the lighting in this kitchen. Or, maybe the solution is room-darkening drapes over every window. And my head.

Growing old gracefully is a lie. No one has ever left fish in the fridge for two weeks and then said, "This fish has grown old gracefully." No, they say, "What the heck is this stinkin' thing doing here? Which is pretty much what I said to my computer screen today. I mean, this just isn't fair. I lost weight this year. Doesn't that guarantee celebrity looks? Turns out, the celebrity I most resemble is Gollum.

Oh, wait… I almost forgot that I'm writing something spiritual here. Okay, well—the bad news is, I'm very old. The good news is, I'm dying. And by that, I mean a new and improved me is on the way.

1st Corinthians chapter 15 tells us we don't know what we'll look like because our physical body is merely a seed, and only when it's put in the ground will our new body emerge. Just like an acorn doesn't resemble the majestic oak tree, our body doesn't resemble what we will be.

Like a baby in the womb looking down the long dark tunnel thinking, "How can I be sure there's life after birth?" We, too, have trouble wrapping our minds around the idea of life after life. But Jesus said, "Don't let your hearts be troubled. Trust in God, and trust also in Me. There's more than enough room in my Father's home. If this were not so, would I have told you that I am going to prepare a place for you? When everything is ready I will come and get you, so that you will always be with me..." (John 14:1-3).

Come quickly, Lord, I'm goin' to seed here.

…Our earthly bodies are planted in the ground
when we die, but they will be raised to live forever…
1 Corinthians 15:42

They are buried as natural human bodies, but they will
be raised as spiritual bodies…
1 Corinthians 15:44

For our dying bodies must be transformed into bodies
that will never die…
1 Corinthians 15:53

20

Travel Insurance

I drove to the thrift store for some extra teaspoons and, as always, after a bit of hunting, found exactly what I needed: a jean jacket. I love it, especially for travel. It goes with everything (except the mustard recently spilled on it). It's comfortable, and, most importantly, has large inside pockets that hold travel documents on the right, and money on the left, so all valuables are tucked against my body. A thief has to go through me to steal them.

So it is with our lives. If we belong to God, we can absolutely trust in his safekeeping. 1st Samuel 25:29 says, "You're life is safe in the care of the LORD your God, secure in His treasure pouch."

Years ago, our lives were threatened by a violent gang. Fear paralyzed me. I couldn't sleep, eat or focus on anything but the threats we received, so I memorized scripture: Psalm 91, Psalm 40, and many other verses promising protection.

One night, trembling with fear, I saw a vision of myself planted in the palm of God's hand; yet still I felt exposed—as if in the flat of his hand, I was held up for the world to see. But then Jesus gently placed his other hand over me as a cover, sheltering me as one might tenderly hold a baby bird. I was not only kept; I was hidden in His hands.

If you have made Jesus your Lord, no danger can touch you without first passing through Him. Read Psalm 91 aloud when you are tempted to succumb to fear. He's got you covered.

"Hide yourself in God, so when a man wants to find you he'll have to go there first." —Shannon Alder

The LORD says, "I will rescue those who love me.
I will protect those who trust in my name."
Psalm 91:14

Those who live in the shelter of the Most High will find rest in the shadow of the Almighty.
Psalm 91:1

21

FIND ME ON ~~INSTAGRAM~~ MY KNEES

I love social media. While searching for a rye-based sour-dough starter recipe, I found an excellent how-to video on Mongolian throat singing.

I "heart" every new job and potty-training success, connect cross-country with kids and grands, and pray for the sick and struggling. But I don't take the bait on posts like, "Let's see who my real friends are..." (Apparently not me.) or "I think I know who'll repost this..." (Ad infinitum, ad nauseam.) I scroll past the latest Mark of the Beast theories, delete wealthy Nigerian relatives (obviously, we aren't related; I have detached earlobes), decline invitations to play my life away on Candy Crush.

Jesus said, "Follow Me." Not "Follow Me on Instagram." I remind myself of this in the fog of early morning, when social media lures me like cinnamon rolls at the mall. But temptation takes no captives here as I click on my Bible app to view today's Verse of The Day which is... "How to Spot a Real Narcissist." Aaaack! I did it again!
Now for the actual Verse of the Day: Proverbs 17:24: "Sensible people keep their eyes glued on wisdom, but a fool's eyes wander to the ends of the earth."

Boy, ain't that the truth. The thing is, there IS no end to all those tips on recognizing a toxic relationship (like, for instance, the one between me and social media).

I wonder if the Book of Life records time spent on our phones. Here's an idea: Let's stop calling them iphones. Let's call them iforgottolive.

Translation: Carpe Diem before Diem Carpes You.

Social Media is not going away, so Lord, help me use it to promote good, to pray for others and share Your Word. As one social influencer said way back when scrolls were the media of choice:
FOLLOW ME as I FOLLOW CHRIST.
#PAUL #FIRSTCORINTHIANS11:1

My heart has heard you say, "Come and talk with me."
And my heart responds, "LORD, I am coming."
Psalm 27:8

Listen to my voice in the morning, LORD. Each morning
I bring my requests to you and wait expectantly.
Psalm 5:3

22

OH, RATS!

I spent part of my childhood living on a small ranch southeast of Oroville, California. Though money was scarce, we seven kids remained remarkably healthy due to the abundance of raw milk, fresh eggs, and gallons of root beer Kool-aid.

One sizzling summer day, we noticed the Kool-Aid had an odd smell. Beneath the sticky-sweet chemically-induced artificial taste we loved so much was essence of gym socks. My brother's investigation revealed the source: a rat practicing the back-stroke in our well. It's astounding how a smidgeon of rat can ruin a good day.

I envision a parallel situation in my spiritual life. Sin may seem molecularly insignificant, but rodents of pride, judgment, resentment, and stinkin' attitude poison my heart's wellspring.

When I raise a prayer chalice to the Lord, brimming with praise and petitions, I wonder; does a heavenly host ever sound an alarm,

"Don't drink the Kool-Aid— I smell a rat!"

Light and heat are often used to make infected water potable. So too, as I yield to the light of truth and the heat of conviction through the Holy Spirit, I am made pure once again.

Even with diligent guards in place, this long hairy tale is a constant of life. Thankfully, the Holy Spirit never wearies of repeating, "Gear up! Rat in the water!"

Guard your heart above all else,
for it is the wellspring of your life.
Proverbs 4:23

Don't you realize that this sin is like a little yeast
that spreads through the whole batch of dough?
1 Corinthians 5:6

23

Working Out the Harmonies

Before automatic dishwashers, there was singing. Kitchen duty for our family of nine fell to my sisters and me. One scraped and stacked the dishes, another washed, and another, with dishtowel in hand, feigned busyness. (I had a hang-nail, oKAAAY??!!) This was the usual M.O. unless one of us had been caught saying "Shut Up," in which case the chore was mine alone. (As you can imagine, we devised brilliant alternatives like "Shut Ut" or "Up Shut," but my mother wasn't stupid.)

We sang as we worked. The songs came to us via our two eldest sisters. We younger kids were in awe of their bubble hairdos, matching sweater sets, and any songs emanating from that mysterious place of higher education: High school in the '60s.

With damp muslin dishtowels as props, we twirled through the myriad of pots, pans, and songs, honing both housekeeping and musical skills. The genre was insignificant—we sang everything; mostly uplifting tunes like, "Poor Man Lazarus, sick and disabled…" Our singular interest was creating beautiful harmonies.

Practicing three hundred and sixty-five evenings a year at our kitchen venue created an ear for notes. Eventually, upon hearing a melody, we'd know the 3rd and 5th harmonies like the back of our Melmac™ dishes.

Over the years, music became our identity, the anthem of our family gatherings.

Not long ago, I encountered a gal taking professional harmonizing lessons. I'd never considered it a subject of study. I knew little of music theory; harmonies came naturally, didn't they? Hadn't our ability been honed simply by living together? Of course, there was a hidden learning process: finding the complementary note, learning to "stay in our lane" despite the notes trilling all around us. We focused only on that sweet spot of knowing we'd gotten it right, holding the last clear note into eternity, awed by the beauty of perfect harmony.

I've been thinking lately about Romans 12:16 and 1 Corinthians 1:10, which command us to "live in harmony with each other." To live in harmony doesn't mean we all sing the same notes; we sing complimentary notes. We may even sing dissident notes as long as tension is eventually resolved. We may not sing simultaneously, but wait for our part. We listen, fit in, and yield to others singing their part.

Learning to live in harmony is indeed a process, whether in the kitchen, marriage, the church, or with the guy next door. But when we get it right, it's music to God's ear.

May God, who gives this patience and encouragement, help you live in complete harmony with each other, as is fitting for followers of Christ Jesus.
Romans 15:5

Live in harmony and peace. Then the God of love and peace will be with you.
2 Corinthians 13:11

24

Fixer Elixer

There's no human as insecure as a teenager in angst, except for the mom attempting to help them. Their hurt scared me, and when I'm scared, I talk. And when terrified, I talk more—and louder, like maybe I can scare fear away with volume: BOO! …Yeah, that works.

Pin-size problems became large, family-size with the help of my fumbling platitudes, weak analogies, and fake cheeriness. My attempts to pacify, edify and mollify were met with a double dose of rolling-eye. In summary, my problem-solving skills are equal to that of Mr. Bean.

So I turned to the only thing I knew would help; the Mother-of-All-Sure-Fixes, that magical Fixer-Elixer (Kids, fill in the blank here ____); that's right: Tea. On the opposite side of every slammed door soon lay a tea tray, that silent symbol of "I'msorryican'thelpyoueventhoughIwanttobutI'materriblemothersothiswillmakeitallbetter…"

Whenever my mind screamed, "CLEAN UP ON AISLE 5!" I'd whip out my tea and start pouring, hoping that cup, saucer, milk, and sugar would somehow equal truce and love.

I'm kind of a package deal: antagonist, protagonist, mother, and teenager. But, like the two tiny tubes that make up superglue, put them together, and your thumb and finger will be permanently stuck together. Okay, not the analogy I was looking for.

Thank God they had a father.

John is ever the reasonable one. He's "Let the dust settle" to my "Let's make a tornado!" He's the calm sea of "Lord help us…" to my storm- waving, "GOD HELP YOU!"

Thank God I have a Father.

No matter what is happening in this crazy, mixed-up world, God, through His son Jesus, desires to meet with crazy, mixed-up me.

To the unreasonable, He says, "Come let us reason together…" (Isaiah 1:18 NKJV).

To minds that say, "There is no way to find truth in this life," Jesus says, "I am the Way the Truth and the Life" (John 14:6 NIV).

To those who don't believe, Jesus says, "I am the author and completer of your faith" (Hebrews 12:2).

To the heartbroken who say, "Yeah? Where were YOU?" Jesus says, "I cry too." (see John 11:35)

On the other side of every slammed door, He waits, holding out the cup of salvation, saying, "Take and drink." But two-fisted drinking is prohibited. "I drank, and it did nothing," she says, with the Lord's cup in one hand and a tarot card in the other. The Bible says, "You can not drink from the cup of the Lord and the cup of demons, too. You can not have a part both in the Lord's table and the table of demons" (1Corinthians 10:21).

Or, as the book THE HELP so aptly reveals: Poop in the pudding destroys the pie.

The Lord offers the true antidote for my crazy, so why would I drink it with a chaser of insani- tea?

I will lift up the cup of salvation and
call on the name of the LORD.
Psalm 116:13 ESV

Then he took the cup of wine and gave thanks to God
for it. Then he said, "Take this and share it
among yourselves."
Luke 22:17

25

LOOMING LARGE

I woke up dispirited, saturated with doubt—like a wet cat in the rain. Even my morning brew seemed to chug, "You THOUGHT you could, You THOUGHT you could..." Yet out of habit and obedience, I washed my face and shuffled out to the kitchen to begin my morning reading with a Verse of the Day: "Arise! Shine! For your light has come, and the glory of the LORD shines over you" (Isaiah 60:1).

He had me at "Arise!"

In the original Hebrew, *arise* literally means: "Get up! Stand up! Do the thing. Establish the work and carry it out."

The second word *shine* means "be light and give light." Also, "lighten up" — Ha! WORD right there.

Your light has come means, "♪Here comes the sun,♪ do-do-do-do...here comes the sun...♪" Or literally, "*the dawning of scattered rays, as of the sun.*"

And the glory of the LORD shines over you. What looms large over you? Whatever it is, God's glory—i.e., all His resources, and all He is, looms larger. HE IS IN THIS, and HE IS WITH YOU.

The first thing on my "To Do" list is very doable: "Be still and know that He is God."

And now, ARISE! DO THE THING!

I may be a cat in the rain, but the Lion who Reigns is with me—and with you, if you'll have Him.

God has spoken plainly, and I have heard it many times: Power O God, belongs to You...
Psalm 62:11

O my people, trust in Him at all times. Pour out your heart to him, for God is our refuge.
Psalm 62:8

26

HOW SWEET

"Is there anything you need from the store?" John asks as he pulled on his coat.

"Umm…yes…I need powdered sugar to frost these." I say, eyeing the baking sheets of cookies sitting on the counter. "A one-pound package will be more than enough." He comes back with eight pounds of powdered sugar.

This is typical of my husband. We've been through this before:

"I'll never use a pound of sage before it goes bad."

"Five dozen eggs for the two of us, *really*?!"

"What am I going to do with three pounds of butter?" (Make more cookies, of course.)

His "more is better" motto ruffles my efforts to organize what little storage we have, but then I think, "Okay, maybe he's not the most practical, but he is most generous." He's never accused me of spending too much (even when I have). And never once in fifty years has he said, "We just can't afford to pay tithe this month." In seasons without steady income, he continues giving generously to the Lord and others.

I've been a happy recipient all these years, so why make a big deal over the pallet of toilet paper?" It's not like *that* will go unused.

Note: this had nothing to do with *The Great T.P. Shortage of 2020*. Our supply was stocked way before then (and he won't let me forget that stroke of genius anytime soon).

As I look for a place to put the seven pounds of extra powdered sugar, I start thinking about this lavish spending. Isn't that what God does for us? James 1 says God gives wisdom lavishly to those who ask for it, not eking it out according to I.Q. or our most recent performance. He gives generously without finding fault.

And what about mercy? Jesus never says, "But I just gave you some yesterday." No, "His mercies are new every morning"— fresh baked, fragrant, and ready upon our awakening.

In addition, the more we give away what He's given, the more bountifully He provides, as we're told in Luke 6:38: "Give, and you will receive. Your gift will return to you in full—pressed down, shaken together to make room for more, running over, and poured into your lap. The amount you give will determine the amount you get back." Wow.

We are recipients of one openhanded gift after another. A quick study of creation tells us He didn't scrimp, but made plentifully, beautifully, and tenderly. And, was there anything practical, anything *but* lavish about God coming in newborn-size to a barn, flanked by a bunch of filthy animals (and a few four-footed creatures as well)?

The powdered sugar will eventually run out, but until then, it will be a reminder of God's "impractical" and overflowing love every time I see it next to the five cases of root beer stashed under our couch.

My purpose is to give them a rich and satisfying life.
John 10:10

See how very much our Father loves us, for He calls us His children, and that is what we are!
1 John 3:1

27

SMOKIN' HOT

He's charming, attractive, and thrives on dangerous behavior and self-exaltation; He's a master manipulator whose relationship goal is maximum control. Yep—Satan is a psychopath.

He was the most beautiful of all God's creations, the star of the show. He had access to all of heaven—the beauty, resources, and music; all but one thing: Control. In his determination to usurp God, he and his fellow protesters—a third of the angels —were forced to find new territory. Thus a beautiful day in the neighborhood ended tragically for Eden (Isaiah 14; Ezekiel 28).

Jesus says Satan's goal is to rob, kill—and not content with that—to destroy (John 10:10). Like fire burning through the same place twice. He's okay with me believing Christ died for me as long as he can cast doubt on God's present goodness to me; me in my "special circumstance." Satan strokes my head and coos, "Yes, yes, God's Word is true generally, but your situation is unique; you're broken."

Excuse me?!? Last I checked, this whole world is broken, and that's why Jesus came.

We may recognize something is not right – something "otherly" to the devil's lures, but we're free (indeed!), so we naively hold the match as he lights up.

As Daniel Walsh said, "It feels like heaven to flirt with hell." Take a hard look at addiction and broken marriages and tell me it's not true. Satan didn't die for you; he's determined to have you die for him.

"There is no neutral ground in the universe; every square inch, every split second, is claimed by God and counter-claimed by Satan." —C.S. Lewis.

There's only one way to defeat the devil, as modeled by Jesus: "GET OUT OF HERE, SATAN" (Matthew 4:10).

So humble yourself before God.
Resist the devil, and he will flee from you.
James 4:7

But when people keep on sinning, it shows that they belong to the devil, who has been sinning since the beginning. But the Son of God came to destroy the works of the devil.
1 John 3:8

28

Taking The Cut

I'm not good at hair, so except for a wedge cut, thanks to Dorothy Hamill circa 1980, I keep my hair long. I have mastered the "mess" aspect of a messy bun, but that's about it. I did receive a compliment in '94 for my French braid tuck. The boys at the kitchen table cheered, "Mom! Your hair looks so cool—just like the face of an alien!" ...Not quite the look I was going for.

To grow long hair, it must be trimmed regularly to promote healthy growth and remove weak strands, yet it seems counterproductive to the goal. I wince at the inches of "perfectly good" hair lying in a pile on the floor.

In the same way, God runs a salon of sorts. Jesus says His Father removes things from our lives to produce growth. These are often "good" things, productive things, even things we do for Him.

At "Shear Heaven Salon," these cuts include people who add joy and strength to our lives, people we count on, maybe even "enthrone" or place on a pedestal, like Isaiah's friend and supporter, King Uzziah. Isaiah says, "In the year King Uzziah died, I saw the LORD, seated on the throne..." Uzziah dethroned revealed the LORD enthroned, launching Isaiah into a new perspective, obedience, and fresh ministry (Isaiah 6).

I have cried private tears over the snip, snip, whack from the Scissors of the Lord. But in that sorrow, I've experienced His gentle hand and voice saying, "Wait… just wait… new growth is coming. I'm making room for healthier, fuller, more productive growth."

When I yield to His clippers, fresh beginnings result. I may not understand the "why" this side of heaven. But someday, as David said to the Lord, "I will be satisfied with seeing Your likeness" (Psalm 17:15, NIV).

I am the true grapevine, and my Father is the gardener.
He cuts off every branch of mine that doesn't produce
fruit, and he prunes the branches that do bear fruit
so they will produce even more.
John 15:20,21

For I am about to do something new.
See, I have already begun!
Isaiah 43:19

29

Change It Up

"We're sorry; we don't speak Whinese. Please go to your room, and come out with a cheerful attitude or on your twenty-fifth birthday, whichever comes first." This was the general response to any of our kids exuding a cloud of moodiness due to chores. Chores were required, and all ten of us were familiar with the verse, "If you don't work, you don't eat" (2 Thessalonians 3:10 CEV), as that was our family policy. Hunger is quite inspirational, and in a short time, attitudes changed. Simply put, they responded with repentance.

We sometimes complicate the words of Jesus; repentance is one such word. In the original language of the Bible, it means "to have a change of mind," including opinions and responses to people and circumstances—and ultimately to God. Repent means to turn from sin, especially our "darling sins," those pet behaviors of self-pity, self-focus, blame, and resentment. Foremost, we need a change of mind regarding Jesus and His authority over us. Is He Lord, or isn't He? Just as a misbehaving child was denied participation in family activities, our self-serving behavior detaches us from God and His design for our lives.

Jesus says, "Change your mind, change your ways." Repentance is required, yet we're not expected to go it alone. Occasionally, when one of our children was told to adjust their behavior, they would say, "Help me—I can't stop myself!" How sweet was this expression of need! It made me love them even more, if that was possible. I would set them on my lap, and together, we'd talk about it, pray for help, and help would come.

So it is with Christ. Repentance is a choice and a gift. We choose to receive the gift from God. 2nd Timothy 2:25 says, "Opponents must be gently instructed, in the hope that God will grant them repentance leading them to a knowledge of the truth." The word *grant* is literally "gift".

As with every family, whether ours or the church's, unity and productivity are restored when we turn from our opinions, attitudes and actions and seek God for His.

The Lord bought us shoes of repentance; our part is to throw away the old pair and walk in the new.

And I will give you a new heart, and I will put a new spirit in you. I will take out your stony, stubborn heart and give you a tender, responsive heart.

Eze.36:26

"Repent and turn from your sins. Don't let them destroy you! Put all your rebellion behind you and find yourselves a new heart and a new spirit. For why should you die? I don't want you to die," says the sovereign Lord, "Turn back and live!"
Eze. 18:30

30

Don't Forget to Remember

Our young son played the role of private consultant to his little brother. One morning as they sat at the art table, he offered counsel on how to avoid parental discipline:

"Don't tell them you forgot to obey; they'll have to discipline you to help you remember. Instead, say you didn't hear them."…Smart kid.

I, too, used the excuse, "I forgot!" to brush off careless behavior until I observed a friend's child who selectively "forgot" every task or rule. It was maddening to watch him at this game. Eventually, his friends were few, and invitations fewer. God used him to convict me of my own frivolous attitude and helped me find creative ways to remember stuff. Forgetting isn't as benign as the word implies. The down-range effect of some things forgotten can be disastrous. I'm referring to spiritual forgetfulness, a common theme in the Bible:

- "You forgot the God who gave you birth" (Deuteronomy 32:18).
- "Watch yourself that you do not forget the Lord who brought you out of slavery" (Deuteronomy 6:12).
- "Let all that I am praise the Lord; may I never forget the good things He does for me" (Psalm 103:2).

The word "forgot" in the Bible can often be translated "mislay," like the card intended for my sister but hidden on my desk until half-past her birthday. It wasn't lost, but buried under the debris of life. So too, activity, complacency, and enticements can cause us to mislay our purpose; forget for whom and for what we live.

Spiritual dementia doesn't happen overnight. The slow slide begins when we forget to thank God for all His benefits—like air, for instance; and working body parts.

Minor ingratitudes become major bad attitudes.

But He's forever calling, encouraging me to remember my first love. I can't say I didn't hear Him.

I, yes I, am the one who comforts you…
yet you have forgotten the LORD, your Creator.
Isaiah 51:12a,13a

Go back to what you heard and believed at first;
hold to it firmly. Repent and turn to me again.
If you don't wake up, I will come to you
suddenly, as unexpected as a thief.
Rev. 3:3

31

FEAR OVERBOARD

Due to the storm, ours was the last boat permitted to leave the dock. We were heading out to a village church on a small island in the Philippines. The wind pitched the boat this way and that while waves surged over us. Wiry sailors tight-roped over the riggings— grasping, tugging, and shouting to each other across the deck in their native tongue, which I interpreted as, "I thought you said this boat couldn't sink!" Finally, one of them cut the anchor line.

Like Jesus in the storm, I reclined in the boat. Unlike Jesus, a silent scream froze on my lips. If I've told the Lord once, I've told Him a thousand times, I don't want to die in water unless it's a hot tub and I'm already asleep.

My mind plays scary music when I'm frightened, usually an organ piece in minor keys, but this time I heard the score from Jaws: DundunDUNdun…But then snippets of another song from Psalms rode across the wind,

"Where can I go from Your presence, O Lord…even in the depths of the sea, you would still be there to guide me…"

Would Christ be with me even at the murky bottom? Yes, we have His Word on that. Together we'd dog-paddle to heaven, if necessary.

Taking my "what ifs" to the nth degree and envisioning

Christ even in THAT place is the "Peace! Be still!" my scaredy-cat self needs.

Eventually, I heard another sound: a multitude of security alarms blaring as waves pummeled the cars waiting on a ferry at the dock. The DOCK! We're safe! Though quite late to the Sunday morning service, no one seemed to mind the delay or our bedraggled appearance. Least of all me. I was just glad to appear.

When you pass through the waters, I will be with you…
Isaiah 43:2 ESV

You go before me and follow me. You place your hand of blessing on my head…if I go up to heaven, you are there… if I go down to the grave, you are there. If I settle in the uttermost parts of the sea, even there your hand will guide me and your strength will support me.
From Psalm 139.

32

WHITE-WATER WISDOM

While white-water rafting on the North Fork of the American River, we headed toward a roaring gorge where the water churned like a sea monster with a bad tooth. Suddenly this twenty-ish kid (young enough to be my son) jumped out of the raft into the water. I did the only sane thing a mother would do: I jumped in after him.

Turns out, that was *in*sane. I went under the tumult, and every time I surfaced, I gulped water rather than air. So sure of my eminent death, my mind actually started singing, "Amazing Grace, how sweet the sound…I once was lost but now I'm drowned." As I flailed, I heard a still, small voice saying, "Head to shore! Head to shore!" It wasn't God's voice, but it was a good second—the voice of our rafting guide.

I was so busy flailing and trying to "save" the other guy (who didn't need saving after all) I forgot to swim. Also, had I remembered the life vest wrapped around me, I wouldn't have panicked, knowing regardless of the depth to which I sank, I'd be buoyed up again.

These lessons apply not only to white-water rafting but to navigating through news that a loved one has jumped the ship of faith. It's normal to freak out when your spouse or child takes a dive; you just can't REMAIN freaked out. When you stop flailing, you'll remember to swim. You can't save 'em. There's only One who can, and our Guide is very aware of the situation. Leave it to the Expert.

Remember your life vest, wet suit, and scuba gear, which hadn't been invented back in the day of Ephesians chapter 6, but they had "the full armor of God." You have that. Put it on. Learn to use it.

There's no greater classroom than the School of Hard Walks, and no greater guide than the One Who's seen it all. Last I looked, He was not wringing His nail-pierced hands, but rather holding them out to you— yes, YOU. Take hold. Trust. Learn. And don't forget to breathe.

Put on every piece of God's armor so you will be able to resist the enemy in the time of evil. Then after the battle, you will still be standing firm.
From Ephesians 6

The waves of death overwhelmed me; floods of destruction swept over me…But in my distress I cried out to the Lord…He reached down from heaven and rescued me; He drew me out of deep waters
2 Samuel 22:5,7

33

RESET

My phone seemed sluggish, unresponsive, and then it crashed. John suggested a reset, so I turned it off and, after a couple minutes, on again. Now with my phone restored, I'm happily back to the land of pocket calls, nostril photo bursts, and insulting people via Siri texts (note to Siri: I'm bringing "hors d'oeuvres," not "horse ovaries" to the church potluck).

A verse from Psalm 23:3 came to mind, "You restore my soul, you lead me in paths of righteousness for your name's sake."

Restore my soul means to bring back, return, and refresh the self-life, i.e., my appetites and passions, the activity of my mind, will, and character.

He *leads me in paths of righteousness* means to be directed and re-directed in the right way to go.

I need the daily reset of Christ to unstick me from self, to awaken me from unresponsiveness, and pick me up when I crash. We are told in Isaiah 55:6 to "Seek the Lord while He may be found, call on Him while He's near." It's not that He distances Himself, but I do. So before getting stuck, sluggish, or crashing, I read His Text daily for a reset. It's a good call.

Restore to me the joy of your salvation,
and make me willing to obey you.
Psalm 51:12

After you have suffered a little while, He will restore, support, and strengthen you, and He will place you on a firm foundation.
1 Peter 5:10

34

A Picture Of Life

Over 250 people have died taking selfies. Social media researchers have coined the word "killfies" to describe this phenomenon. We shake our heads at the story of the one who trespassed the jaguar barrier, stood too close to the burly-headed bison, or hand-fed the bear. But here's the thing; over half the women who died taking selfies were NOT engaged in high-risk activity. They died because, while focused on that little rectangular image of self, they did not consider the unexpected; a gust of wind, the slam of an ocean wave, or the crack of a thunderbolt.

Jolts, shocks, and rip-tide life events are not only possible, but probable and pending, as by-products of living here on planet earth. Yet anticipating unknowns only creates anxiety, and fearing what may happen tomorrow kills today, so where can we find peace?

In Matthew chapter 7, Jesus likened our lives to one of two houses. We're not told what they look like, but in my imagination, they overlook Malibu Beach. They may well appear identical until a storm hits; then one remains, while the other crumbles right off the cliff. The storm revealed the difference: one house was built on bedrock, the other on sand.

In 1980, a perfect storm hit our lives. Waves of terror and despair held me underwater long enough to scour away the rubble in my life. When I emerged, one rock remained, and I held fast to it, not by the strength of my trembling arms, but by the strength of that rock: *The Lord my Rock.*

I didn't know if our lives would be spared, but I became convinced that Jesus would be there for us, even if the worst occurred.

Since that first episode, every cliffhanger has reminded me not only I can, but I MUST trust the Lord my Rock, not based on feelings, but by faith, recalling His ability to save me from my selfie and the photo-bombs of life. No wind, wave, or thunder catches Him off guard: He commands them—and comforts me—with, "Peace! Be Still!"

…My God is my rock in whom I find protection.
He is my shield, the power that saves me,
and my place of safety.
Psalm 18:2

[Jesus said] "Anyone who listens to my teaching and follows it is wise, like a person who builds a house on solid rock. Though the rain comes in torrents and the floodwaters rise and the winds beat against that house, it won't collapse because it is built on bedrock. But anyone who hears my teaching and doesn't obey it is like a foolish person who builds a house on sand."

Matthew 7:24-26

35

Protection From Deadly Vermin

We're serving at a church in Central America—also known as the bug capital of the world—so my signature scent these days is mosquito repellent. My morning routine consists of heading out to a wooden swing to read, pray, and slap. I've tried slathering myself with essential oils, but the buzz in the mosquito community is they love the extra sauce.

Now it's full-on chemical warfare. So far I've found three brands guaranteeing 99% effectiveness, but with a hundred billion mosquitoes a.k.a. "microvampires", that other 1% works out to be…uhh…let's see…I don't know… taptaptaptap…one billion.

I've learned smoke is a deterrent. This fact is brought to us by experts who, through numerous studies, have determined that virtually all mosquitoes are non-smokers.

Worse than mosquitoes is the "Doctor Fly." This is your basic yellow horse-fly but with various letters after its name. John got hit by one—twice, actually. The first time, it "bumps" to anesthetize the skin (thus the name; and no, I'm not making this up), then it returns to complete its residency at Johns-Topskin. Thankfully, with a catapulting flick of his finger, John expelled the flying dermatologist before it finished its rounds.

Yet we have much to be grateful for: Though they eat us, they don't lay eggs under our skin. As the bug experts so gently explain, "While the doctor fly uses live flesh for blood meals, they lay eggs in decaying matter." …We're old, but thankfully not THAT old.

We'll save the discussion of scorpions, sand fleas, and what entomologist academia refer to as "No See'ums" for another time. Suffice it to say, "Repellent: don't leave home without it."

Though mosquitoes are considered the most dangerous of all animals due to the diseases they carry, it occurs to me, as I read through the book of James, that I've been host to other vermin of greater destructive potential: Biting words that sting those closest to me (James 3:1-12); Creeping attitudes of cynicism and ingratitude that eat away foundations of faith and love with termite-like persistence (James 1:14,15); And, the generalized buzzing of fears, whose bite paralyzes with, "I can't trust God in *this* situation." (James 5:7-18)

The Bible warns us of things that seek out unprotected hosts in which to lay eggs and reproduce until decayed matter is all that's left. The combination of three repellants: the Word of God, prayer, and obedience, must become our signature scent. But these are only effective with the main ingredient: a relationship with the Living Christ, Jesus. Those who know Him find His love covers and protects from all that would destroy our soul. Guaranteed, 100%.

In the same way, the tongue is a small thing that
makes grand speeches. But a tiny spark can
set a great forest on fire.
James 3:5

Temptation comes from our own desires, which entice
us and drag us away. These desires give birth to sinful
actions. And when sin is allowed to grow,
it gives birth to death.
James 1:14, 15

36

How To Avoid A Crash

When it comes to mountain driving, I'm an expert at being scared out of my wits. So the idea of navigating through the mountains to my speaking engagement prompted me to pray for a cancelation, like maybe a volcanic eruption. This may seem overkill, but why pray for sickness? This is a Christian conference; everyone will pray for healing, and I'll be back to driving through the mountains.

Well, as it happened, a friend of a friend who flies offered to fly me in his light plane; I was elated. I climbed into the plane like a farm dog with his nose out the old truck window, fur whipping and tail wagging, basking in the pleasure of a new adventure. The harsh majesty of granite walls, crags, and summits dotted with icy lakes loomed so close I could almost touch them.

The seasoned pilot guided the plane through a course for the most scenic views and least turbulence (still enough to set this dog whining and almost peeing). Twice an alarm sounded to warn us to increase altitude—we were too close to a peak—and of course, the pilot heeded the warning calmly but quickly.

I considered what it would take for the plane to crash. It wouldn't take the whole massive mountain to bring disaster;

a mere fragment of rock from some peak, connecting to a fraction of metal on the plane, would be enough to bring us down.

So it is with the temptation to sin. As the book of James warns regarding our words, one tiny spark is all it takes to set the whole forest (our lives or the lives of another) on fire. In reality, MOST temptation only needs a spark to ignite it to full-blown sin and the ensuing disaster.

Concerning my flight, I'm thankful the pilot was not lax in dealing with the warning alarm. He didn't merely say, "God, please remove the mountain," or "Lord! Please don't let us hit that summit!" Well, maybe he *did* under his breath. But he immediately pulled up and MOVED out of the way.

While there is a time to pray, "Lord, remove this mountain," more often, we must be the ones to "re" move— move in another direction, which is another way of saying, "repent."

The only way out of temptation is to flee. In Genesis 39, Joseph, when enticed by Potiphar's wife to have an affair did, not say to himself, "I'm strong, I can handle this…" or "I'm sure if I meet with her over coffee, I can help her understand why this wouldn't be appropriate." Heck no—he freakin' *FLED*! —so fast that she was left holding the clothes she'd torn off him. There's no such thing as harmless flirting with temptation. Pull up and pull out—MOVE (or remove)—

whether it be the siren song of a "slight" indulgence, an inclination to self-pity, an impulse to speak your mind (apart from the mind of Christ), or flying in a little too close for a better view.

Stay the course. Safe landings, everyone.

Run from anything that stimulates youthful lusts.
Instead, pursue righteous living, faithfulness, love,
and peace. Enjoy the companionship of those
who call on the Lord with pure hearts.
2 Tim. 2:22

But Daniel was determined not to defile himself…
Daniel 1:8

37

Full Of It

The problem with junk drawers is, they're so good at their job. Mine needs cleaning out regularly, and by "regularly" I mean whenever the scissors and tape give the stapler a wedgie, forcing me to use my official junk-drawer de-jammer: John's iPad stylus, which I usually return (but if not, just rummage through that drawer there, John).

I put off cleaning this drawer because each item represents a decision, and a hundred decisions is too much brain energy, and…of course, there's the guilt: Take this tiny LEGO covered with unidentifiable junk-drawer crumbs, for instance. My grandchild's success as an architectural designer could depend on that minuscule blue block; yeah, that's right—the one his grandma threw out.

And this metal thingy I found on the kitchen floor last year. Statistics prove it will reveal its vital role in the operation of a thousand-dollar appliance the moment the garbage truck drives away.

Okay—well, this expired coupon for JCPenneys that went out of business last year can be tossed for sure. Except…the back of this coupon is blank, and when the recession hits, I'll need paper to write the list of groceries I can't afford.

I've learned the best way to handle this all-important First World and—-let's be honest—Third World problem ("Do tribes in Papua New Guinea have junk drawers?" You ask. Of course they do! They keep their trinkets in those handy gourd pouches they wear as "drawers" below the waist).

Where was I…oh yes…the junk drawer solution: After removing the few actual necessities, I dump the rest into a box to be tossed, or picked through during harrowing car trips to distract me from all the other cars swerving toward our—WATCH OUT!!—lane in our 25 m.p.h. town (I have those issues, too).

Well, today I woke up with a junk drawer full of worries jamming my brain. I told John about it this morning, to ask for prayer, but also as a warning because as a professional junk dealer, I'm living proof of the validity of Psalm 37:8,

"Fret not; it only tends to evil".

In the original Hebrew language, this can loosely be translated, "When she's fretting, irritability at obnoxious sounds such as breathing, is to be expected." John's wholehearted prayers at such times are exceptional. And after the "fervent prayer of a righteous man," I read today's verse from Psalm 55:22 in the Good News Bible:
"Leave your troubles with the Lord and He will defend you; He never lets honest people be defeated."

So I listed all my fears to the Lord (writing them down so that I could remember what I was supposed to forget) and then envisioned the junk drawer. I removed the few items needed for the day, and boxed up the rest, handing it over for the Lord's safe-keeping or to toss as He sees fit.

Now I can get on with those few needful things today. First on the list: Thank John for his constancy in prayer. And thank the Lord for being keeper of the Junk Drawer.

But the Lord said to her, "My dear Martha, you are worried and upset over all these details! There is only one thing worth being concerned about. Mary has discovered it, and it will not be taken from her."
Luke 10:41,42

Peace I leave with you; my peace I give you. I do not give to you as the world gives. Do not let your hearts be troubled and do not be afraid.
John 14:27 NIV

38

JUST WAIT

I couldn't wait to get home. We flew into Reno, spent the night, and woke early, anxious to cover the long miles. The morning was still dark as I put the final items in my suitcase. I finished with a satisfying ZZZZIP and hummed a little going-home song. But with one glance out the window, my face fell as quickly as the snow outside. It was beginning to look a lot like Christmas in the worst way. Usually, we're not concerned about driving in such conditions, but our rental car came fully equipped with bald tires that slid like Disney on Ice.

We paced back and forth—Well, I paced while John click-click-clicked on local TV stations, hoping for just one renegade weatherperson with something nice to say. After pulling up every map, app, and hap-less forecast, we asked the Lord for His opinion. Do we take a chance and get on the road? Stay another night at the hotel and try to get some work done? Both John and I sensed the answer was, "Just wait."

Wait is my least favorite word in the English language—and I doubt I'd like it any better in Italian or Swahili. Actually, it's not the word I hate, but the definition: *"to delay an action until something else happens."*

Ugh. I shrugged off the urge to punish the weather with a counter-storm of bad attitude and traipsed down to the lobby with John. Food helped. Thanks to the motel waffle maker, I loaded up on carbs in preparation for tomorrow's marathon—the 1.5K I'm walking (maybe not tomorrow, but soon).

Within a few hours, we were in the car and on our way. The drive home was blissfully boring, punctuated only by gunshots, thanks to Louis L'Amour and Utah Blaine on Audible. We rode into the sunset and set our baggage down in the living room before dark, thankful for the Lord's guidance, grateful we'd listened, and for the reward: HOME.

This got me thinking about the whole WAIT thing. Much of life is waiting—or not waiting and getting myself in trouble as a result; an impatient heart leads to imprudent action.

What if we *did* wait? Waited to respond. Waited to learn how to love, rather than quit loving. Waited to develop a better approach to things and people; waited for a better "me" to emerge from the lessons learned. What would our lives look like if we trusted in the process God designed for us? Just as a child in the womb develops over a given time frame, God has a time frame for our development and maturity. Maybe if we were not so quick to abort, we'd come through the tunnel into abundant life.

We are not couch potatoes in God's waiting room. Not idling, but bridling our impatience into prayer as an exercise of trust, knowing God will work.

God waits for us, unruffled. I want to learn from Him. There are 85 verses with the word "wait" in the English Standard Version of the Bible, many of them telling us how, why, and the resulting benefits, and also the dangers of impulsiveness. So, what are we waiting for?

Wait for the Lord. Travel steadily along His path
and He will honor you by giving you the land.
Ps. 37:34 (ESV and NLT)

Consider the farmers who patiently wait for the rains
in the fall and in the spring. They eagerly look
for the valuable harvest to ripen.
James 5;7

It is good to wait quietly for salvation from the LORD.
Lamentations 3:26

39

LITTLE FAITH

While ruminating over unanswered prayers, and by "ruminating," I mean pounding my pillow and imploring God to "DO SOMETHING!" I remember a petition from years ago: Our 3-year-old son, Micah, was given a little red tricycle for his birthday. One day, it was stolen from our yard. From then on, his bedtime prayers included a request for the return of his tricycle.

Initially, his dad and I prayed with him in this, not only because we couldn't afford another, but moreover, we wanted our son's faith in God to be reinforced by answered prayer. But after the first year, we gently dissuaded him from praying for that trike, "Uh, yeah, son…about that… here's the thing…" But he'd have none of it and continued for three long years.

Walking to the park one day, we found the tricycle sitting just around the corner from our house. Since none of our neighbors had young children, we surmised whoever took it felt remorse and dropped it off near where they'd stolen it. Though it had been painted over, we could still make out the stenciled letters of our son's name on the back. Although now too big for the bike, he jumped around with gratitude, high-fiving the Lord for this answered prayer. I was humbled by my son's faith.

I think God brought this to memory today because I, too, am experiencing the sadness of things stolen and lost. I'm reminded to pray and to pray, and KEEP. ON. PRAYING.

As F.B. Meyer said, "The greatest tragedy of life is not unanswered prayer, but unoffered prayer." Jesus commands us to pester Him with prayer (Luke 18:1-8) and not give up. The answer may be just around the corner.

One day Jesus told his disciples a story to show that they should always pray and never give up...
Luke 18:1

Continue steadfastly in prayer, being watchful in it with thanksgiving.
Colossians 4:2 DBY

40

SWEET LIFE LESSON

"Come on over this evening for Phil's birthday celebration," my friend said. "We're having Oreo cookies and milk."

I'm not a fan of Oreos, but we love this family and the birthday boy, so John and I accepted the invitation. Considering I'd gained a few pounds on a recent trip, I was happy for a dessert so easily resisted.

On the drive to their house, I mused, "OREOS— Really? Is this a thing with Millennials nowadays?" A question revealing not only the age of our friends but my date of birth and place of origin: last century and some other planet. I learned a lot last night.

Lesson One is that I should stroll the cookie aisle more often. Much has changed since 1970. Store-bought cookies aren't generally my thing, so I've lived in utter ignorance regarding this cookie brand. I'd heard of double-stuff and mint joining the blackish chocolate outsides. Still, I had no idea the variety was equal to an entire cereal aisle. Imagine my surprise when set before me on the birthday table was a display of Oreos as far as the eye could see (true, I wasn't wearing my glasses at the time, but still...). In addition to the standard fare mentioned above, the celebration included Chocolate Peanut Butter Oreos,

Cinnamon Bun Oreos, Strawberry Shortcake, and Cookies 'n Cream— which I find ironic since the original Oreo is, in fact, cookie WITH cream is it not?

Our hosts displayed great restraint and tolerance in withholding guffaws as I expressed amazement at the diversity. They patiently led us through the rigors of Oreo 101, which, as it turns out, is actually Oreo 85. There are eighty-five varieties, including Pina Colada, Kettle Corn, Wasabi, Coke (with actual fizz), Special Edition 4th of July Firework Oreos (with a mildly exploding filling), and the family favorite: Easter Peeps-filled Oreos.

Lesson Two revealed further proof of my unenlightened state. Until last night, I considered cookies a finger food, so you can imagine my confusion when I was handed a fork. Being from the Stone Age, I turned that metal pronged-thing over and over in my hands, pondering its purpose. Then I recalled what I do when invited to the White House —Or WOULD do if ever I was invited: I waited and watched. After the birthday song, each family member stood an Oreo on its side like a wheel, pierced the creamy part with their fork, and set it into their glass of milk.

"Wait until you see a little bubble—that means it's ready," said one child genius.

Kids these days; not only can they hack into our computers, they know their Oreos. I followed the instructions, and experienced nothing short of euphoria. The formerly dry and tasteless outside morphed into soft cake with—get this—frosting *inside*! Wait. You KNEW about this and didn't tell me?!?

In conclusion, Peanut Butter's my favorite, hands down…no—I mean Cinnamon Bun. Wait…make it a Double.

This "Epic Evening of Oreo Awesomeness" reminds me of a Bible verse: "How great is the goodness you have stored up for those who fear you. You lavish it on those who come to you for protection, blessing them before the watching world" (Psalm 31:19).

Every day as we ask the Lord to reign over all we are, all we have, and all we do, we discover His master plan, resources and adventures beyond our wildest imagination. Jesus came to give abundant life, custom-crafted and flavored by He who created us all, including Sam J. Porcello, the inventor of the Oreo.

My people will feast on my good gifts.
I, the LORD, have spoken!
Jeremiah 31:14

No eye has seen, no ear has heard, and no mind has imagined what God has prepared for those who love Him. But it was to us that God revealed these things by his Spirit.

1 Corinthians 2:9

41

Tribal Mentality

"I'm such a Loser," I sigh as I close the book about a missionary in Papua New Guinea whose husband was murdered by a member of the tribe for which this couple had spent twenty-four years translating the New Testament. She stayed to finish the work, resulting in an outpouring of the Holy Spirit in the area.

And then there's me; I only speak one language unless baby talk counts. She knows how to use a machete. Maybe I can learn— I'll check my phone for a machete app. This woman does laundry using her feet while I'm drying the polish on mine.

I lay on the bed pondering my sorry state and praying for God to help me. Apparently, He heard me 'cuz this ticker tape played across my mind:

"Okay—let Me get this straight—this is about YOU. And unless you serve some yam-eating, gourd-wearing tribe and John gets axed in the head by a psycho, you have no value? Are you an atheist? Because your god is too small to be real. Are you ungrateful for the life I've laid out for you; discontent with the calling I've chosen for you?
"Are you telling the Potter how to shape the clay?"
Have you not heard, 'To *obey* is better than sacrifice?'"

Ummm…Yes—I mean—-no. Alright. I'm better now. I'm sorry, Lord. I'll just get up and make this bed for You and do the next thing You say to do, and the next, and the one after that…

"Satan is the author of all 'do-it-yourself' spiritual enterprises." —Warren Wiersbe

…Do you seek great things for yourself?
Seek them not…
Jeremiah 45:5a ESV

"What is that to you? You follow Me!"
John 21:22

Jesus turned and said to Peter, "Get away from me, Satan! You are a dangerous trap to me. You are seeing things merely from a human point of view, not from God's.
Matthew 16:23

42

BE BOULDER

According to Rock and Ice magazine, Bishop, California, our former home, is the epicenter for bouldering. Bouldering is that insane sport of rock- climbing without ropes, harnesses, or your mom yelling, "Get down from there before you hurt yourself!"

Those crazy kids say it emerged from mountain climbing in the late 90s, but I say it was around way before that. Records of the earliest "dirtbags" (as boulderers lovingly call themselves) date to a thousand years before Christ. In 1st Samuel 14:6, the young adventurer Jonathan said to his young armor-bearer, "Come on-climb right behind me, …so they climbed up [the cliff face] using both hands and feet…" The purpose of their bouldering was greater than the bouldering itself; it was to whip the Philistine thugs, rescuing God's people from bullying.

The sports of bouldering, running, and the majority of Olympic skills have utilitarian origins; they were a means by which something more significant than the sport itself could be accomplished. But over time, the first goals are often forgotten. I'm reminded of a team of men dedicated to water search and rescue, but the group morphed from rescuing people to what is now known as a rich man's recreation: The Yacht Club.

Relating this to life, I wonder what "greater thing" I am missing. Today is Sunday, so I'm considering the "sport" of church attendance. Do I attend church because it's the right thing to do (I "have to" because I'm a Christian)? Is my goal to meet my needs, be around like-minded people, listen to an inspiring message, or promote mere Christian values rather than to glorify Christ? These motives aren't wrong as recreational sports go, but Jesus died to save us from being recreational Christians.

Our purpose for anything we do in the name of Christ is to know Him better, to live by His power rather than our effort, and to learn the grace of suffering with Him (Philippians 3:10). Living in Christ is a challenging climb, but one that empowers us to love our spouses, children, in-laws, and out-laws, and be His hands and feet to a world struggling under the boulders of life. Jesus calls us, as Jonathan did,

"Come on— climb right behind me…using your hands and feet."

> And he said to them, Follow me,
> and I will make you fishers of men.
> Matthew 4:19 ESV

> …The GOAL of our instruction is love.
> 1st Timothy 1:5

43

SCREETCH, PRAY, LOVE

She was a walking set of fingernails, and I was her chalkboard. You know the kind; every time she opened her mouth, screechy-scratchy screeeeetch…I tried to avoid her cat claws, but she backed me against the wall every time. I became wacky with anxiety at the mere thought of the next encounter.

So I began to pray for her. I mean, REALLY pray for her. Not "God give her headlice and chickenpox so she'll have something else to scratch;" but, "Lord bless her. Whatever is at the root of her behavior, meet her need, and show me how to love her and demonstrate that love in a way she can receive."

Over time, you would not believe the change: encouragement replaced suspicion, cheerfulness replaced angst, and joy replaced fear.

Oh- I'm not talking about her–I have no idea if she's changed or not. I only know I am no longer the hard surface her nails need.

So I was freed…to love her.

But I say to you who hear, love your enemies, do good to those who hate you, bless those who curse you, pray for those who abuse you…
Luke 6:27 ESV

…because He's kind to the ungrateful and evil.
Luke 6:35 ESV

Be merciful, even as your Father is merciful.
Luke 6:36 ESV

44

I Hear it Now

I sat with my four-year-old son, Tim, quietly gazing up at the night sky.

"Look at all those stars..." I whispered.

"Yes— I can hear them," he whispered back.

"You can *hear* them?" I asked.

"Yes..." He said. "...They sound like crickets."

Until that moment, I was deaf to the crickets, but now the cacophony couldn't be ignored. How weird something so obvious was beyond my acknowledgment.

In the same way, my recognition of God—His nearness and HERE-ness is sometimes overlooked. I can be so consumed by a singular aspect of life— especially in the dark hours, I'm oblivious to His presence and voice until I intentionally listen for Him.

Knowing He is with me and actively engaged in every detail of my life changes how I view my situation, allowing me to see beyond the temporal to the eternal. As the song from Casting Crowns says, "Things aren't falling apart, they are falling into place."

I'm learning to listen for the sound of the Lord in the dark of night.

But if from there you seek the Lord your God,
you will find him— if you seek him with all
your heart and with all your soul.
Deuteronomy 4:29

And they heard the sound of the Lord God walking
in the garden in the cool of the day…
Genesis 3:8

My heart has heard you say, "Come and talk with me."
And my heart responds, "Lord, I am coming."
Psalm 27:8

45

PART OF THE PRIDE THING

Well, here we go again.

This week John addressed a list of nasty habits for me to consider. Okay—a list of one, which is the same as a hundred, and he didn't exactly call them nasty, but I read between the lines. He spoke kindly, and I responded similarly: "Kindly suck it up." To my credit, I didn't say that out loud.

His concerns were of a spiritual nature, and I wanted to retaliate: "Oh Yeah? Well, guess who left their underwear on the floor today?" But I kept my cool. Very cool. Downright COLD.

As it turns out, he was being overly-sensitive, judge-y, and critical. Oh no…wait…that was me. It took a while, but I repeated to him what I thought he was saying until I was 100% sure he was wrong, and then we prayed.

I wrestled all day in prayer. Wrestled with God. Apparently, John had managed to convince even God of my sin. And they won. They won because truth wins, and this truth from the Gospel burst to the surface of my murky little heart:

"He must increase, but I must decrease."

"He" being Jesus.

This verse from John 3:30 shredded my paper-thin defenses, motives, and questions. John was right—both Johns were right. But even if my John had been wrong, the truth of this verse would have worked right things in me. If my life's goal is truly, "More of Jesus, less of me," this brings an end to the parsing out of just how much responsibility I'll accept for my attitudes, motives, and actions because one thing is for sure: I must take full responsibility for my sin of pride, and its many disguises of which I am still ignorant.

Later that day, I thanked John for sharing hard stuff with me, acknowledged my failing, and asked him to keep praying for me.

Battle Done. Freedom Won.

Back to being the happiest couple on earth.

This "being made more like Christ" is not for sissies. I want to resist it. But in the end, I find Jesus irresistible. (And John too.)

But speaking the truth in love, we are to GROW UP in all ways into Him who is the head–Christ.
Ephesians 4:15

As iron sharpens iron, so one person sharpens another.
Proverbs 27:17

And just in case I'm ever tempted to start parsing:

Why not just accept the injustice and leave it at that?
1 Corinthians 6:7

46

THE SANCTIFIED CARROT

"Lord, this is your idiot servant speaking. I don't think I hear Your voice. I thought I did. But now I'm thinking I don't and…have I ever? I know you are 100% reliable, but I'm 100% idiot, so why would you even bother? Maybe You DID want me to become a nun after all, but then who would have taken care of John and the kids?"

This was last week's prayer after what I thought was an open door slammed shut.

Enter, John a.k.a. The Voice of Reason:

"Laura, I believe we did hear the Lord. I also believe in the 'sanctified carrot.' Sometimes the Lord puts a carrot before us to get us moving in a particular direction and then changes the course. He knows we wouldn't budge if that juicy carrot wasn't offered. Once we're out in the open field and the gate closes behind us, He can direct us more readily into His will."

"Humph." I said, "But I even thought he gave me a Bible verse as confirmation."

"Well, He knows you look to His word for direction. It got you moving, right? Let's just keep seeking Him, and trust that He will show us the next step."

It still looks like the Red Sea is comin' up, and those crazy Philistines are clattering in my head, but I'm feeling a little less tweaked and trusting the Lord to guide. I have His word on that.

"In all your ways acknowledge Him and He will direct your path" (Proverbs 3:6).

Whether you turn to the right or to the left,
you will hear a voice behind you saying,
"This is the way. Walk in it."
Isaiah 30:21

She turned to leave and saw someone standing there.
It was Jesus, but she didn't recognize him.
John 20:14

47

CALL GIRLS

My sister Karen and I talk on the phone every week. It started years ago when we both needed encouragement. She was sick, and I had a bad case of teenagers. So, across two states, we helped each other rise up and walk. Our problems were each other's much-needed distraction. As mutual counselors, we offered profound words of support and wisdom like: "Oh my gosh!! Are you kidding me? You poor thing!!" With each rehashing of our personal angsts, the clouds lifted until we could see Our Father, Who Art in Heaven. And guess what? We came through. Soaked to the skin with mascara running, we pulled each other along and made it home to the fire.

We still talk weekly, discussing internal affairs such as Holiday dinner menus for low-carb, high-maintenance guests; hot topics including shiny versus dark baking sheets (we took a poll over the phone; the results were two out of two in favor of the dented, discolored thrift-store variety); and debating the scientific hypothesis for why peeling a potato towards your body is faster and more efficient than peeling it away from your body. We laugh uproariously at our common depictions of life's insults and injuries, we listen, nudge each other toward the Truth, and sign off.

After our good-byes, we go about the business of doing the next thing, with the knowledge someone on the other side of speed dial is cheering us on to the finish.

Isolation leads to a hardened cynicism toward life, people, and, ultimately, God. The Bible tells us so and gives us the remedy, "Encourage one another daily, as long as it is called Today, so that none of you may be hardened by sin's deceitfulness" (Hebrews 3:13).

We are each other's sisters, blood or otherwise. Pick up the phone, go to lunch, and practice your listening skills. It's your call, girls.

48

A Short(s) Lesson in Humility

After the birth of our fifth child, I was happy to be back in "normal people" clothes. One sunny day, I pulled on a pair of shorts, and to my surprise, they fit. I turned this way and that before the mirror, very pleased with myself as we all set off for lunch at the park. An hour later, after a stop at the park restroom, the kids ran ahead to find the perfect picnic spot. I lagged behind carrying the usual truckload of gear and noticed people giving me a second look. I smiled and thought, "Yeah, I look totes adorbs in these shorts."

I was setting out the pb&js when a young girl approached and said, "Excuse me, ma'am, you have something on your back." I twisted around to look, and there, plastered to the back of my shorts, was a paper toilet seat cover.

Two verses come to mind, Daniel 4:37 and James 4:6:

"And those who walk in pride he is able to humble." Yeah, no kidding.

"God opposes the proud, but gives grace to the humble." Like I don't have enough opposition in my life? I need to add GOD to that list?

I've not worn shorts since.

When pride comes, then comes disgrace,
but with the humble is wisdom.
Proverbs 11:2 ESV

The Lord lifts up the humble;
he casts the wicked to the ground.
Psalm 147:6 ESV

49

Unsolved Mysteries

As John was leaving for church one Sunday morning, he grabbed his shoes by the front door and slipped them on. He came out to the kitchen and said,

"There's something wrong with my shoes; one of them is too small!"

"What?! That can't be—you wear them every Sunday!" I replied.

"I know—but look; one *is* smaller than the other."

To my amazement, one shoe appeared to be a half-size smaller. After cogitating way too long, we laughed at the weirdness of this mystery, and he found another pair of shoes to wear that day.

Mysteries. Life is full of them. Things that just don't make sense. If we could view them from the top of the universe, we'd say, "Oooooh, so *that's* what happened." My husband John imagines Heaven will have an IMAX screen in which we'll see behind-the-scenes action films. Like "This Was Your Life," or "The REST of the Story," or "~~Un~~Solved Mysteries." Until then, I trust.

It's nothing much to ponder the minor mysteries of disappearing shoes, but some of the biggies in life can really hang us up. The list of "whys" stretches to eternity.

Many things just don't make sense this side of Heaven. Am I willing to admit I have a finite mind that will not and can not understand? Can I be content entrusting those unknowns to the God I do know? I expected it from my children; can I do the same as a child of God?

We solved the mystery of John's shoes. Earlier in the week, we'd hosted a worship night at our house for a large group from our church. They all dropped their shoes at the door, and somebody accidentally took John's shoe. That somebody had the larger shoe, and hadn't noticed the difference of the roomier fit. The mystery was eventually solved, and the shoes were exchanged, but it took a while.

So, too, the Lord allows us to know the answer to some mysteries, and we are privy to some secrets (though not nearly as many as I'd like) as we follow Him. It's one of the many benefits of obeying His Word. More times than I can recount, we've been forewarned of things to come and instructed on what action to take. But I'd freak out if I knew it all, which is probably one reason God holds His cards close.

Lord, help me be content to act upon the mysteries You have revealed and entrust You with all the rest.

I no longer call you slaves because a master doesn't confide in his slaves. Now you are my friends since I have told you everything the Father told me.
John 15:13-15

The LORD our God has secrets known to no one. We are not accountable for them, but we and our children are accountable forever for all that he has revealed to us so that we may obey all the terms of these instructions.
Deuteronomy 29:29

But it was to us that God revealed these things by his Spirit. For his Spirit searches out everything and shows us God's deep secrets.
1 Corinthians 2:10

50
His Eye is On Jack Sparrow

"We don't lick the bottom of our shoes," I say as we begin story time. You can tell I'm a preschool teacher by my classroom rules. I try to keep things simple, but I forget to mention a thing or two on the first day of school.

In any case, there's always a student whose goal is to see how many rules can be broken. This little guy thinks I'm oblivious to the Lego man slipped into a pocket, a horn snapped off the plastic triceratops, or the puzzle piece forced through the heater vent.

I have a particular affinity for little rascals—as I am one myself—so I try to encourage, remind them of rules and consequences, and exchange elaborate high-fives for any movement in the right direction. But if a child is bent on destruction, I limit their access to activities and items that may be stolen or damaged or cause them or others harm. The covert removal of freedoms goes unnoticed, but their world is a tad smaller than it was yesterday.

The Bible addresses those who think God does not see, or misconstrue His silence as approval. God does see, but most often, He allows His created natural laws, such as *cause and effect* (sowing and reaping), to take their course. He wants to save us from ourselves and the destruction around us, but He'll not force our compliance. Instead, He sends warnings, engineers damage control, "safeguards the Legos," and sets boundaries. We may be free agents in rebellion, but that perceived freedom denies us abundant life.

God's forbearance should not be confused with poor eyesight. He's seen it all, winces, and sometimes…cries. "His eye is on the Jack Sparrow, and I know He watches me."

> When you did these things and I kept silent,
> you thought I was exactly like you. But I now arraign
> you and set my accusations before you.
> Psalm 50:21 NIV

> "The Lord isn't looking," they say, "and besides, the God
> of Israel doesn't care." Think again, you fools! When will
> you finally catch on? Is he deaf—the one who made
> your ears? Is he blind—the one who formed your
> eyes? He punishes the nations—won't he also
> punish you? He knows everything—doesn't
> he also know what you are doing?
> Psalm 94:7-10

51

I Once was Lost, But Now I'm Phoned

My idea of a Hi-tech gadget is an iron with a retractable cord. There are no words to describe how horrible I am with tekkie things. I lose my phones. I drop them in toilets, throw them across parking lots (as I toss my granddaughter her flip-flops), leave them at out-of-town restaurants, and drown them in pools and oceans. I forget passcodes and security answers.

John just spent two hours with the Apple tech guy, reconfiguring my new phone because I'd forgotten all my pertinent information, but never once did John roll his eyes or say, "Are you some kind of idiot that you give me five possible answers to the security question, 'What was the name of your first pet?'"

When the problem is finally resolved, he hands me my shiny new working phone, and what do I do to show my appreciation? I drop it with a hard smack on the floor. Silence, then he quietly says,

"Laura, take care of your phone."
Not with visible restraint, just kindness.

I literally cried and laughed and cried at my stupidity and his goodness. I'd be living in the dark ages, but for John,

my Tech Redeemer. John rightly could've said, "Laura, you don't deserve a new phone." He'd be right, yet he loves me enough to give me one anyway.
That's grace.

It got me thinking of the Bible describing our sorry human condition of failure, sin, and death and then breaking the despair with this phrase: "BUT GOD…"
"We were dead in sin, BUT GOD…made us alive in Christ…" (Ephesians 2:1-4).

"BUT GOD will redeem me from the power of the grave, and He will receive me" (Psalms 49:15).

"BUT GOD is judge…" (Psalm 75:7).

"BUT GOD knows your heart…" (Luke 16:15).

"BUT GOD chose the foolish…" (1Corinthians 1:27).

"BUT GOD…comforts the downcast, and comforted us…" (2 Corinthians 7:6).

"BUT GOD had mercy on…me also…" (Philippians 2:27).

"BUT GOD shows his love toward us, in that, while we were still sinners, Christ died for us" (Romans 5:8).

There are too many BUT GOD's to list here, but if you, like me, recognize your utter hopelessness to be anything or do anything other than fumble and fail, remember

"BUT GOD…"

52

RUNNING FREE

Our seven-year-old Annie was learning to ride a bike. Struggling to stay sunny-side up, she'd weave between trees and parked cars like a drunken sailor as I shouted, "Look OUT! Don't run over Mr. Rude's leaf pile!" (A coveted landmark of our neighborhood.) and, "Pedal faster!" Of course, to her little mind, if she couldn't control the bike going slowly, how could the answer be, "Pedal faster!"? But she obeyed, and it worked. She flew a block and a half and returned.
Nailed it.

I recall a scene from a classic movie in slow motion, Annie dismounting starry-eyed, like an astronaut returning from the moon, helmet under one arm waving to her cheering crowd of one with the other. Together we rode to the park. She pedaled her little Kermit the Frog legs to break the sound barrier. Her blond curls an aerial banner proclaiming, "Land of the free! Home of the brave!" Her face radiating joy and amazement at accomplishing the impossible; she'd discovered what aviator John Gillespie Magee meant when He penned these words:

"I have slipped the surly bonds of earth and danced the silver skies…"

There is an "Annie Sensation" that occurs in the spiritual realm. That glorious freedom: running in obedience to God. David says to the Lord in Psalm 119:32, "I run in the paths of Your commands, for You have broadened my understanding."

Sometimes I think, "How can I run in His paths when I can't even walk in my own?" But when I trust that He knows even more than stuff like "pedal faster," and I do what He says in His Word—not partially, but wholly—I behold the aerial view, and I "slip the surely bonds of earth…"; the surely bonds of self.

A true Free Spirit is one led by the Holy Spirit. And like the writer of "High Flight,"

"I put out my hand and touch the face of God."*

Anyone who chooses a life of sin is trapped in a
dead-end life and is, in fact, a slave. But if the Son
sets you free, you are free indeed!
From John 8:36

You have been called to live in freedom, but don't use
your freedom to satisfy your sinful nature. Instead, use
your freedom to serve one another in love.
Galatians 5:13

* Read the poem and the story behind the "High Flight" by aviator John Gillespie Magee. It's a great depiction of our life in Christ.

53

Content Mint

I'm making a watermelon-feta- mint salad, which got me thinking about mint. It grows wild in a stream behind our home. I love the fragrance, freshness, and the stepping-into-coolness to gather a bundle; and what *is it* about something growing wild? I will throw a few watermelon seeds next to the mint to keep it company. With dairy cows nearby for cheese, I'm dreaming of a ready-made salad.

Back to the mint: It's just there, year after year, doing the hula to the music of the stream, looking beautiful. It doesn't grunt or strain to grow; it doesn't uproot itself in a panic during dry spells; in fact, it has quite an extensive root system, cultivated, I suspect, in the years of drought this valley has endured. The plant drinks what's given, and the outcome is inevitable: growth, leaves, reproduction, repeat. Its minty greenness is a vibrant contrast to the dried thistle soon-to-be tumbleweed in this desert valley.

I started thinking about the comparison of two lives described in Jeremiah 17. The first belongs to the person who trusts in human potential, his own and others. He is described as a shrub in the desert, living but thirsty, always seeking more, and in the end, parched and dried up. The second illustrates the person who relies on the Lord: "Like a tree planted by water, that sends out roots by the stream and does not fear when heat comes, for its leaves remain green, and is not anxious in the year of drought, for it does not cease to bear fruit."

We who live in Christ don't have to invent growth. "In Him we live and move and have our being," stated the apostle Paul. It's a done deal. We simply plant ourselves in the abundant stream of everything He is and stay put.

Droughts and heat will drive our roots down, and there, in the deepest darkness, we discover the crystal waters, the subterranean things of Christ, revealed only in those times of secondary growth.

Dwelling in Christ, we dance the hula in the stream of His love, bear fruit, reproduce, offer what we have to others, and repeat.

It was mint to be.

They are... planted in the house of the Lord; ...even in old age; they bear fruit and are fresh and flourishing.
Psalm 92:13a,14a

The Lord will continually guide you and satisfy your soul even in drought...and you will be like a watered garden...
Isaiah 58:11

He who delights in the Lord and his instructions will be like a tree planted by the river that brings forth fruit in season; his leaf will not wither; and whatever he does prospers.

Psalm 1:3

*Watermelon-Mint-Feta Salad

Combine in a large bowl:
1/3 c. oil, 3 Tablespoon lemon or lime juice, 2 teaspoons salt, 1 teaspoon hot sauce (optional), 1/2 teaspoon pepper. Add: 1 cup coarsely chopped mint, 1 small red onion, diced, 8 oz. feta cheese, crumbled, and 1 cubed or balled seedless watermelon (8-10 cups). Chill and serve.

54

Fairest of All

Soon the sweet smell of cotton-candy, snow cones, and cow manure will waft across this little community. Big rigs filled with colorful fiberglass animals are parked on this side of town. Today the Ferris wheel is up, so I'm perusing the County Fair booklet for the "must-see" attractions and music venues and—of course, the latest in deep-fried food (the term "food" is used loosely here). New to the "heart attack in a paper cone" list are the following deep-fried delicacies: bubblegum, pop-tarts, S'mores, and Cadbury eggs—all music to my little heartburn. For you more nutritiously-minded, there's deep-fried Club salad.

I find in myself the little kid jumping up and down with delight at the remembrance of bumper cars and tilt-a-whirls of years past. OK, yeah -that was me slumped over the side of the squirrel cage at age seven, vomiting pink popcorn onto the people below, but I'd begged my friend Cindy to stop twirling the cage, so it was NOT MY FAULT!
Ah, the memories evoked by a county fair. The mere anticipation keeps me energized. Soon I'll be inhaling the sights and sounds of All Things Fair.

In the spiritual realm, I experience a much deeper anticipation when contemplating heaven. I'm not talking about the twisted version of naked harp-strumming cherubs (who look like they've eaten a few too many deep-fried Snickers bars). I'm thinking of the real heaven, where all lying, hating, hurting, and emaciation by addictions or cancer will be gone forever. Where every longing- be it laughter, love, or quiet, is fulfilled, and people from "every nation, tongue and tribe" (Revelation 7:9) will be gathered at His place. Just think of the music from THAT cultural festival! And the food will be to die for; The Marriage Supper of the Lamb will be out of this world.

When I see the signs of Jesus comin' to town, I think about all He is, and the anticipation keeps me going strong. We don't know everything about heaven; the Lord wants us to love Him for Who He is-not for the prize behind Door Number One; plus, there'd be a stampede bigger than Walmart's Black Friday if we knew all that heaven held. So I focus on the "here" with an eye for "there."

But if the beauty of creation, what I know of Jesus, and His presence in my life is any indication, heaven is worth the wait, and the cross of Christ has already purchased the ticket. Pick it up now for the great adventure. Soon we'll be inhaling the sights and sounds of Fairest Lord Jesus.

You must be ready, because the Son of Man will come in an hour when you do not expect him.
Matthew 24:44

No one knows the day or the hour, not even the angels in heaven nor the Son, but only the Father. As it was in the days of Noah, so it will be at the coming of the Son of Man. For in the days before the flood, people were eating and drinking, marrying and given in marriage, up to the day no enter the arc; and they knew nothing about what would happen until the flood came.
Matthew 24:36-38

For the price of sin is death, but the free gift of God is eternal life through Christ Jesus our Lord.
Romans 6:23

55

Today's the Night

My friend texted me last night to tell me to go outside and look at the moon, so I did. The stars were exceptionally bright against the deep blackness. Initially, the mountains hid the moon, but I could see the glow coming as if from a sunrise. I stayed there, breathing in the light, until it dawned on me that I witnessed this glorious light because I stood in darkness.

We often hear voices of hopeless doom and gloom for the days in which we live, and I've been known to join that chorus. But last night was a reminder that today we have the most incredible opportunity to shine the hope and joy of our Lord—not in spite of, but because of the darkness around us. This day, this dark day, His stars can display most brightly His Light.

This little light of mine, how will I let it shine?

"Look at how a single candle can both defy and define the darkness." —Anne Frank

…In the midst of a crooked and twisted generation, among whom you shine like the stars in the universe as you hold fast to the word of life.

Philippians 2:14-16a

Give thanks to Him who made the heavenly lights…
the moon and the stars to rule the night.
His faithful love endures forever.
Psalm 136:7, 9

56

Body Heat

Feeling chilled and achy this morning, I held my hands over the stove. The warmth was so comforting I was tempted to roll my whole body over the burner, but the image of that came to mind, and I thought better of it. I did thank God for the luxury of heat as I lingered there.

I had nothing to do with the warmth. I merely went to the source. So it is with all consolations. I can't "muster up" comfort; I need to go to the Source of all comfort. Then, when I've been warmed, I can place my hands on another and comfort them. But that is not enough. The comfort I bring is temporary. My hands will lose their warmth unless I am a conduit of The Eternal Source of Comfort, Jesus Christ.

After experiencing a near-death trauma, I wondered if I'd ever feel "normal," smile, or experience joy again. A young woman living with us at the time helped me, "Well, a *new* normal will emerge, but yes, you will smile again, and you will experience joy."

I could trust her because she'd experienced tremendous violence, yet she knew Jesus Christ as her Comforter and was a humorous, unruffled, and joyous presence in our home. And, of course, she was right.

Thank you, Lord, for using our suffering to draw us to Your comfort. May I not hoard Your comfort to myself but help others find strength in You, as Jonathan did for David. May I take their hand and, together, hold Yours.

...Jonathan went to David at Horesh and
helped Him find strength in God.
1 Samuel 23:16 NIV

"Blessed be the God and Father of our Lord Jesus Christ, the Father of mercies and God of all comfort, who comforts us in all our tribulation, that we may be able to comfort those who are in any trouble, with the comfort with which we ourselves are comforted by God."
2 Corinthians 1:3,4 NKJV

57

Odd Thing, Grief

Inner space is the region between Earth and outer space. Or, in my case, the region between what life was and now is because someone I love relocated to heaven, leaving a black hole and me in this twilight zone. I feel unfastened, mechanical, and muddled, and also I can't seem to stop eating toast. And butter. Sometimes I put the butter on the toast.

I'm not sad; I feel normal. Uber normal. My inner cheerleader pompoms through her usual routine a bit too brightly, her hard candy shell keeping all the melty parts contained, or tries to…I can't tell…because I'm observing all this from outer space, or inner space, or general spaciness.

I do recall having one clear thought this morning: When I don't know what to do, I should do what I do know to do. But I forget what all that is, so I have to rely on muscle memory, which, as it turns out, is a lot like faith.

I get up and read the Bible, though I find myself thinking, "What did I just read?" I pray for people who are hurting because so many are, and it takes little effort to hold their broken hands. I do the laundry and dishes in slow-mo. My son Tim comes to the dishes' rescue, and mine, to cook with me. We talk, sip chai, stare at recipes, make bread and

Singapore chicken stew, inhaling the spices. I sit in the sun with a magazine and thank Jesus. I visit my daughter Grace at her house just to watch her live and take some cues; I invite the kids and grandkids for a barbecue, and I go to church to hug and be hugged. And, of course, there is John the Baptist—my John, baptizing me in his love.

And I lean, not on my own understanding, but on the everlasting arms of my Confident Confidant, the Lover of my Soul. Who, when I ask, "Everything will be okay, right?" answers, "More than okay. Exceedingly, abundantly, more than okay."

Muscle memory is *the act of completing a particular physical or mental task with such repetition that your body learns to complete the task more efficiently, using less brain power.*

When we habitually rely on the Lord, we build muscle memory to help us when the guiles of life and the trials of death fog our vision. We seek and call on Him now, that we may see and recall Him then—and remember how to live.

Seek the Lord while He may be found,
call on Him while He is near.

Isaiah 55:6

Weeping may last through the night,
but joy comes with the morning.

Psalm 30:5

58

CLIMATE CONTROL

People outside the church are rebellious, apathetic, and self-absorbed, while people inside the church are rebellious, apathetic, and self-absorbed. Hmmm...I'm seeing a pattern here. This isn't how it should be, but it's nothing new.

The church climate back in Samuel's day was cloudy with a chance of judgment- 100% chance. The environment hasn't warmed much. The outlook can be downright depressing, and yet...God is calling. He called Samuel, and though Samuel served in the church, "Samuel did not yet know the LORD and the word of the LORD had not yet been revealed to him" (1 Samuel 3:7). Yet God kept calling, and eventually, Samuel got the message.

Samuel could've found plenty of reasons not to serve the Lord; his mentors were doing a pretty lousy job of it. Likewise, my focus can not be on what the rest of the world —or the church— is doing; the question is,

"What am I doing?"

He's calling; He will keep calling. May our response be as Samuel's when he finally picked up,

"Speak, Lord, your servant hears."

That is why the Holy Spirit says, "Today when you hear his voice, don't harden your hearts as Israel did when they rebelled, when they tested me in the wilderness. There your ancestors tested and tried my patience, even though they saw my miracles for forty years. So I was angry with them." I said, "Their hearts always turn away from me. They refuse to do what I tell them." So in my anger I took an oath: "They will never enter my place of rest." Be careful then, dear brothers and sisters. Make sure that your own hearts are not evil and unbelieving, turning you away from the living God."

1 Samuel 3:8-12

59

HERDING DUCKS

I had excellent plans: We'd finish our foreign assignment and be home by Thanksgiving. I'd visit my sister suffering with cancer, spend the holiday with my children, bake pies, roast turkey...oh, the glory of ducks in a row!

But now, I'm considering roast duck— if I can find one. Feathers are everywhere, and no waddle in sight. Wasn't it Sir Walter Scott that said something like, "Oh what a tangle of webbed feet we weave...?"

Ducks, Schmucks. Things fell apart. The night before our flight, I tested positive for Covid. I called around for a doctor, but no clinic would take me because—well, *Covid* — so we lost our flight money. Our foreign assignment was extended another nine months, and I cried in a closet.

I'm delusional in thinking all my ducks in a row will bring peace. Still, I rearrange, chase, grab, and shout, "Hey you! Get back in line!"

I picture Jesus watching, sympathetic and amused, eventually turning to go, saying over His shoulder, "Shoot the ducks. And come... follow me."

But I know what He's up to. He wants to work in me a peaceful heart. I don't WANT a peaceful heart; I want peaceful circumstances because a peaceful heart means I have to change, be agreeable, yield, surrender…and shoot the ducks.

My heart falls to the ground thrashing and ranting, "GIVE ME MY DUCKS!" I fuss, fume, and finally whimper a pathetic swan song, "Must…Have…Ducks…"

Jesus doesn't get His feathers all ruffled when this duck goes astray. He waits, knowing I'll eventually realize there is no peace apart from following the Prince of Peace.

"You can't change circumstances, and you can't change other people, but God can change you." —Evelyn Thiessen

We can make our plans,
but the LORD determines our steps.
Proverbs 16:9

You can make many plans,
but the LORD's purpose will prevail.
Proverbs 19:21

He Himself is our peace.
Ephesians 2:14

60

IRREGULAR IS A VERB

I've been irregular lately, as defined by the dictionary:
/i(r)' regyeler/: adjective
1. Not even or balanced; twisted.

For example, when my scale shows I've lost weight, I don't pay any attention to what my husband John eats. But if the scale insults me with a ridiculously unreasonable number (How could I have gained three pounds? The whole carton of ice cream weighed less than two), or I have to buy a belt extender for my bathrobe, I start obsessing about everything that guy puts in his mouth. He could eat a bacon cheeseburger with extra fries every night of the week with nary a word from me. But suddenly, because *my* buttonholes on *my* shirt won't keep their little mouths shut, I become the authority on what John should or should not eat. This pattern went unnoticed by me until a voice, in lawyer-speak said, "Isn't if a fact, Mrs. Cowan, that on the evening your husband was eating an Almond Joy, YOU were wanting his candy bar, and though HIS pants still fit HIM, YOUR skinny jeans were everything BUTT, and in a fit of insecurity, denial and covetousness, you took your verbal mallet and hit him over the head about HIS eating habits?!?"

"YES! YES— it's TRUE!" I sob, laying my head on the table (drama is my other coping mechanism).

The Moral of the Story: My sins always look so detestable on someone else.

Thankfully, these irregular patterns of mine are always set straight by the Word of God:

Liars hate their victims. Proverbs 26:28

You've been weighed on the scales and have been found wanting. Daniel 5:27

P.S. Dear John, Here— eat my candy bar.

Peter said, "Lord what about this man?" Jesus said to him, "What is that to you? You follow Me!"
John 21:21, 22

If you continue in My word...you will know the truth and the truth shall set you free.
John 8:32

You were called to be free. But do not use your freedom to indulge the flesh; rather serve one another humbly in love.
Galatians 5:13

61

SHEEPDOG

I don't understand all Jesus implies when He calls Himself the Good Shepherd. My familiarity with sheep is quite limited unless you consider the number of times I've watched the movie, "Babe." So I find it helpful to have a friend who is a Good "Dogherd".

My friend Jan is a dog breeder. But in contrast to your run-of-the-puppy-mill breeder, Jan loves her dogs. Her care extends far beyond the clean water/best food/romps in the park routine. She knows their individual needs and bents. For instance, she's keenly aware of the one in her charge who, like the rat in Charlotte's Web, thinks the world is a veritable smorgasbord (orgasbord, orgasbord), so Jan removes anything remotely attainable by paw, snout, tongue or unwitting cohort. She drops everything to assist the fearful one through labor and birth and proves she's in it for the long haul by training the puppies over and over and (sigh) over until they obey commands instantly—an extra challenge because—well, let's just say, rocket scientists are rare among this particular breed.

Jan calls her dogs by name, and they recognize her voice. In fact, she is so connected to her dogs that it's hard for her to view life apart from them, and others may have difficulty relating to her perspective. Case in point: Years ago, when I told her I was pregnant (again), she said, "Why, you're just like my breeder bitch!"

She must've seen the look on my face because later, she called to make sure I knew that was a compliment. For Jan, a fruitful bitch is an excellent thing. Apology accepted. I understand now: Her ways are not my ways. But I'd still really like to be one of her puppies.

Thanks, Jan, for modeling what my Good Shepherd does for me and teaching me to be a good sheepdog.

Thank you, Lord, for providing precisely what You know is best for us. Thank You that when I feel scattered, You gather me. Thank You for holding me in Your arms where I can hear Your heartbeat, feel Your life, and be healed. Thank you for being gentle and strong, giving counsel and guidance to those of us in some role of authority—who have no idea what to do or how to handle our "young" or inexperienced.

He will feed His flock like a shepherd; He will gather the lambs in His arms and carry them in His bosom, and will gently lead those who are with young.

Isaiah 40:11

I am the good shepherd; I know my own sheep,
and they know me…
John 10:14

62

AHH PARENTING...

If only we'd...I should've...Why didn't I...

This is a little reminder to my parent-friends, who suffer from the "guilt that keeps on giving" due to their children's choices. I know two kids who had perfect parenting in an idyllic environment, yet they both rebelled. In fact, they're famous for their bad decision. God was the perfect Father. The Garden of Eden was the ideal environment, yet Adam and Eve tossed it all away for a taste of the Big Apple. And we did too.

The shock is not that some are lost but that any of us are saved.

The same God who rescues us from our stupidity is here for our children. The Lord is able to save us all from ourselves. And our children, too.

Find common ground (two that come to mind are family history and mutual love) and focus on that. Respect their free will as God respects yours (but if we're talking about adults here, let them practice free will under their own roof). Find inroads and bridges to love.

It ain't over yet. Remember, Lazarus was not only dead, he was stinkin' dead, and only then Jesus acted to bring him back to life. It's our business to love and pray, it's not our business to save.

I've yet to see, "Mom Saves!" on a bumper sticker, but *Jesus saves* to the utmost. "Surely the arm of the Lord is not too short to save, nor his ear too dull to hear" (Isaiah 59:1 NIV).

… I know man's heart is bent on evil from childhood…
Genesis 8:21

… God's kindness is meant to lead you to repentance.
Romans 2:4 ESV

For you Lord are good and ready to forgive, and lavish in mercy to all who call upon You.
Psalm 86:5

63

Disarming Robbers

I was almost robbed this morning. Robbed of joy. Thinking things over became overthinking, and I nearly twitched with anxiety way before my first sip of caffeine. The issue, so insignificant as to be invisible to the naked eye, magnified to an outrageous proportion, thanks to a little help from my friends, a.k.a. "thoughts." I even picked a fight with John. Thankfully, he slept through it all.

I started thinking about joy and joy-stealers. I have experienced pure, inexplicable joy in the most unlikely circumstances. Like, when the FBI commenced changing our names and relocating us, but we stayed to serve our newly-planted church; the moment of that decision, joy flooded our hearts. And like the time joy trumped grief as we prayed over a family crisis.

If circumstances don't rob joy, what does?

Unbelief. Unbelief pretty much leads to every dastardly deed in my life. I don't believe God is in control, so I take charge. I don't believe God's Word is relevant to my situation, so I disobey. I don't believe in the absolute sovereignty of God, so I judge others' disbelief. I don't believe God has a plan, so I lick my wounds and take control—HA!— what a ridiculous concept. In that endeavor,

I snuff out one of the most convincing proofs that God exists and lives in me: JOY.

"The Bible is a book of joy. There are 542 references to joy in the Bible. The gospel of salvation in Jesus Christ is a passport to joy. The secret of Jesus was—and is—His inner joy." —S. Wirt

So today, I choose joy because I choose to believe. And in those times when my heart beats to a different drum, I will pray as the desperate father did in Mark 9:24:

"I believe—help me in my unbelief!"

Strength and joy are in His dwelling place.
1 Chronicles 16:27

Do not grieve for the joy of the LORD is your strength.
Nehemiah 8:10

64

THE BIG IF

Seared in my memory is that time I got totally lost in the dark on the back roads of Mt. Ararat—I mean Loomis, California. No amount of horsepower could do what a simple prayer can, such as,"God,ifyouhelpmefindmyway backtocivilizationandflushingtoilets,I'llserveyouinAboriginal Australiawheretheyeatlivelarvaeforbreakfast." (Apparently, this practice has slid past the watchful eye of PETA.).

I suspect Jesus rolls his eyes at my bargaining. He is not into hard-sell tactics or making deals. He's the anti-timeshare salesman. He won't hold us hostage until we say yes to Him; our sin does that. Nor does He wring His hands over our bad choices (although He does weep). He simply says, "IF anyone would follow me…" "IF you hear my voice and open the door…"

Yet He does send frequent invitations— not for His sake, but for ours. "IF you only knew the gift God has for you… you would ask me, and I would give you living water" (John 4:10).

The only "hard bargain" He drives is salvation as a free gift. It can't be earned. Do you get that? Say it. Say it again. "IT CAN'T BE EARNED."

Once we open that gift, we can't help but love Him back by living for Him or, rather, allowing Him to live through us. He's the fuel; we're the tank.

His invitation is to all, coercion to none. It's a big IF upon which to base our lives; it's a one-time choice, chosen daily. So, every morning, I ask myself,

"If not Jesus today, then what 'IF'?"
I've driven too many hard bargains in the wrong direction to NOT know the answer.

Here I am! I stand at the door and knock. If anyone hears my voice and opens the door, I will come in and eat with that person, and they with me.
Revelation 3:20

If anyone acknowledges that Jesus is the Son of God, God lives in them and they in God.
1 John 4:15

65

BeeAttitudes

My mom found what appeared to be a fast-growing tumor attached to the base of my skull. Since "watch and wait" is the modus operandi for moms without medical coverage (or a driver's license or car), she waited a week before further inspection. As it turns out— Whew!— Nothing to be riled about! It was just an engorged TICK BURIED ALIVE IN MY SCALPAAAAAAACCCCKKKKK!!! It all worked out, though. I mean, the tick worked its way out with the help of turpentine, and the bald spot disappeared a few months later.

An interest in bugs has kind of grown on me, and by that, I mean bugs have taken a warped interest in me and, in fact, grown on me. A moth stuck in my ear is an easy fix; just shine a light until it finds its way out of the Earie Canal. But, some creepers are not as easily identified or removed.

Another time, while fishing with my Dad, a bee landed on my nose. It crawled into my nostril and—I'm not sure— but I think it started building a hive. I did an hour's worth of aerobics in the next thirty seconds while my Dad shouted, "Just stand still! Don't move! Look at me!" I wanted to do anything but stand still. Yet, I obeyed and stood as still as a child can, fingers performing the *Riverdance*, eyes fixed on my Dad. At his command, I took a slow, deep breath through my mouth and, with canon-like force, shot that bee into outer space.

I now limit fishing expeditions to the tuna aisle at the grocers. But I'm not alarmed by bugs anymore because nothing beats a layer of insect repellant like five layers of insect repellant.

The world of insects is not unlike the spiritual world. I use a strong repellent when the devil attacks. We're instructed to "Put on all of God's armor so that you will be able to stand firm against the strategies of the devil" (Ephesians 6:11). What are the strategies of the devil? In short, to make me think the worst of God, the worst of you, and the best of myself, and to convince me that God knows little, you know less, and I know it all. Someone once said, "You can't prevent the devil from landing on your nose, but you CAN prevent him from building a hive in it." Actually, that someone was me.

Don't get stung. Fix your eyes on Daddy, not on the bee, and in the mighty name of Jesus and His Word, *OFF!* that sucker back to where he beelongs.

I command you, in the name of Jesus Christ,
to come out of her. And instantly, it left her.
Acts 16:18

For the word of God is alive and powerful
Hebrews 4:12

For the weapons of our warfare are not of the flesh, but divinely powerful for the destruction of fortresses. We are destroying speculations and every lofty thing raised up against the knowledge of God and we are taking every thought captive to the obedience of Christ.
2 Corinthians 10:5, NASB95

66

It's The Little Things that Count

I was cleaning the windows when I noticed them on the sill; little ant thingys. They looked harmless, so I wiped them away. We discovered too late I'd witnessed rebel-force destroyers, a.k.a. termites, flying reconnaissance to devour another of our basement wood beams.

While I stood back admiring my clean windows.

The resulting damage to our home was extensive and expensive.

I can be just as oblivious to erosion in the foundations of my faith and relationships. Slivers of disobedience, sawdust of critical attitudes, particles of pride, and curled shavings of bitterness all add up to what comes naturally: decay and ruin.

In the Song of Songs, we're told of nocturnal creatures nibbling at the roots in the vineyards of Solomon's day. All was well—or seemed so, on the surface. Blossoms promised a future harvest until picnickers discovered the foxes had picnicked first, and age-old vines toppled to the ground.

I'm reminded and warned, that what seems a "given" must be given daily attention. The Bible constantly reminds us to be diligent and to guard our hearts and minds in Christ Jesus.

We can't see roots being compromised, but we can pray as the Psalmist did, "Examine me, O LORD, and try me; Test my mind and my heart." And then listen and respond. It'll save you in repairs.

Jesus, You are the ultimate in pest control. Help me test and exterminate all that would terminate my love for You. And thank you, Lord that nothing is beyond your power to restore.

> Catch for us the foxes, the little foxes that ruin the vineyards, our vineyards that are in bloom.
> Songs of Solomon 2:15

> A little extra sleep, a little more slumber, a little folding of the hands to rest—then poverty will pounce on you like a bandit; scarcity will attack you like an armed robber.
> Proverbs 6:10,11

67

What's Inside?

Mom was moving back to the old home, so my sisters and I were cleaning in preparation for her return. One morning, as we bustled about, the phone rang. It was Mom.

"I forgot to tell you— all my good jewelry is hidden in cereal boxes in the pantry."

Our eyes widened with alarm at this news. Though the pantry was an outstanding hiding place, we were soon out standing by the trash cans, digging through garbage to reclaim those boxes.

Note: THIS WAS NOT MY FAULT! Those boxes were three years past the expiration date! Yes, they were heavier than expected, but I figured the raisins in the bran had petrified to stone.

My sisters managed to reclaim the treasures, and I demoted myself to yard duty.

This reminds me of the verse in Second Corinthians 4:7, "We have this treasure in earthen vessels that this exceedingly great power may be known to come from God and not ourselves."

In other words, we are merely the old cereal boxes holding the diamonds. Anything of beauty or glory comes from God.

Ask my sisters. They knew me when and know me now. They can vouch for what I am and what Christ is in me: Beauty in the beast.

Most of us were no better than fodder for the landfill before Jesus came along. By "most," I mean me, and by "landfill," I mean hell. In fact, one of the names for hell is Gehenna, located south of Jerusalem, which was the city dump and outdoor crematorium of sorts for every kind of decomposing and detestable thing.

Then Jesus dumpster-dived and recycled me. I'm still just a cereal box – expiration date to be announced, but I have a better-than-bling treasure in me.

That is why we never give up. Though our bodies are dying, our spirits are being renewed every day.
2 Corinthians 4:16

Put on your new nature, and be renewed as you learn to know your Creator and become like him.
Colossians 3:10

68

SMALL WORD, BIG CHANGE

Something's changed in the last few years. I've spent most of my adult life *trusting in* the Lord, but now I *trust* the Lord. Gone are my shopping lists slapped on God's refrigerator, and the newsletters sent heavenward with pleading headlines of,

"Only You Can Save This Child (me) From a Life of Despair!"

My trust is no longer merely IN the Lord; my trust IS the Lord. I rely not on prayers answered, but in He *is* the Answer; not that He fixes, but that He is fixed in His sovereignty, grace, love, and justice.

Great confidence and peace have come in putting all things *Under God*. The clutter's cleared, the clatter silenced; a thousand fretful pleas replaced with, "Please…Have Your way in me."

Not that I don't pray. I pray without ceasing. I pray very precisely, but my focus is not on the specifics but on the General, who rules all and truly has the whole world in His hands. This brings freedom, gratitude, security, and joy. I can fully enjoy the fragments because I know the feast will come- if not here, then in heaven.

I don't need the company of answered prayer. I can be alone, in Christ Alone.

Blessed is the man who trusts in the Lord,
Whose trust is the Lord.
Jeremiah 17:7

I have instructed you today—even you—so that your confidence may be in the LORD.
Proverbs 22:19 CSB

69

FACE PLANT

There's a potted plant on the table next to my chair where I spend my early mornings reading the Bible, thinking, praying, and wondering if there's another way to arrange the furniture in this room. The plant sits in a cobalt-blue glazed pot with good drainage. It's been fed, watered, cleaned, given sun, given shade, and generally coddled. I've defended it through bug invasions and cat attacks. Despite this, the plant has never thrived.

This morning, while staring into space, waiting for the screen in my brain to flicker on, my eyes came to rest on this plant. I noted its sad condition for the umpteenth time— its bedraggled leaves, branches leaning over the edge of the pot as if getting ready to heave after a night of bingeing. Just pathetic. Into the silent morning, I muttered, "You stupid plant— I'm throwing you out."

That kinda woke me up. I started thinking about other things in my life that I nurse along, justify, and feed when I simply need to let go, throw away, and clear a spot on the table. Like a bad movie watched to the lousy end (because there must be some redeeming quality), I hold on to a grudge, an indulgence, or a "best kept secret," (as in, "I best keep this a secret"), thinking it enhances my life, when in reality it's taking up space, time and energy. Most significantly, God has said, "Give it up."

So today, I started cleaning. The plant will go to make room for the Tree of Life.

I once thought these things were valuable,
but now I consider them worthless
because of what Christ has done.
Philippians 3:7

For his sake I have discarded everything else,
counting it all as garbage, so that I could
gain Christ and become one with Him.
Philippians 3:8

70

THE LAST THING ON MY MIND

I'm thinking about death. A friend of ours just died, and another friend is beating it back with a big stick of chemo.

Attempting to appease reality, my mind dances and chants around the night fires of grief in all its stages: denial, anger, and- as the drumbeats slow- acceptance. Acceptance not merely of the inevitable but the grueling process of it all. Meanwhile, death sits passively by, blowing smoking into the air, waiting.

My thoughts are mercury scattering in every direction from a broken thermometer. One thought says death can't be that bad. I mean, all my friends are doing it, and those of us who know Christ understand that it's not the end of the world. Okay—it's the end of this world, but life goes on somewhere else—kind of like moving from one room to another. The problem is, I have a lot of people I love in THIS room. Also, I'm terrified of stubbing my toes really, really badly and smashing all my fingers in the door on my way out. I'm pretty clumsy that way.

There are no directives on this "How to Live While Dying" thing (of course, we're all doing that; we just don't know it). But for those who have to keep their job so they can keep insurance, so they can keep having chemo, which makes them so sick they can't keep their job, have it just a wee bit harder than the rest of us. Also, for caregivers and care-receivers, there are very few answers for how to spend quality time (whatever that is) with a loved one, cheerlead what's left of life together, plan an event for which there is no definitive date, transport to doctors, all while seeing to the shoppingcookingmowingbillpayingdusting. Not to mention laundry.

Times all this if kids are involved.

There is no manual for all the incidentals—the stops and starts, fumblings and stumblings to the gates of heaven. But there is Emmanuel, and the poor Guy has gotten more than a piece of my mind lately about all this, which, surprisingly, made room for the mind of Christ to be in me.
Eventually, we who cling to that cobwebby idea of *Jesus Saves* discover it's the steel cable that sustains us even—especially—as our lives dangle over the abyss. Turns out, Jesus is not the blonde-haired wimp so many artists, and our lack of praying, suggest Him to be.

In the afterglow of my night fires, this big red ember remains: "I know Whom I have believed, and am convinced that He is able to guard what I have entrusted to Him for that day" (2 Timothy 1:12 NIV).

And with that, it occurs to me that death is the last of our worries, the final fretful thought to be swallowed up. Not one more thing will keep us awake at night.

Our next dance is at His place.

In the meantime, let's see each other to the door... with a laundry basket under one arm.

There is more than enough room in my Father's home.
If this were not so, would I have told you that
I am going to prepare a place for you?
John 14:2

He will wipe every tear from their eyes, and there will
be no more death or sorrow or crying or pain.
All these things are gone forever.
Revelation 21:4

71

Extreme Sport

An extreme sport is a term for certain activities perceived as having a high level of inherent danger. These activities often involve speed, height, a high level of physical exertion, and highly specialized gear or spectacular stunts. The list includes bungee jumping, cliff climbing, and whitewater kayaking—and get this: something called "Ultimate Fighting."

What could be a more extreme sport and spectacular stunt than that in which John and I have engaged by being in our 50th year of marriage and raising eight kids? The very ACT of marriage calls for highly specialized gear (if you catch my meaning).

Following a two-year-old through the day involves a high level of physical exertion, does it not? John and I have rescued our children from roof peaks, the outside of an escalator headed over a sheer drop from the third floor of Macy's, and placed ourselves in the line of fire (vomit and diarrhea) numerous times, sometimes bribing each other with rare commodities like a couple hours of peace and quiet to "handle it this time." Okay, three hours and a cheesecake.

I'm not even gonna mention the Ultimate Fighting Championships. Which for us consist of short bursts (me) and long sighs (him). Then we pray—okay, truth—I sulk, and *then* we pray. We don't usually go beyond three rounds: talk, apologize and hug.

Even the reasons people engage in extreme sports relate to marriage. Most said they've had plenty of adrenaline-pumping moments. But the real pleasure comes from mastering the rush and conquering challenges by developing skill and composure over years of experience.

Through fifty years, we've rafted through greater than class 5 whitewater in our patched-up rubber raft named, "To Have and To Hold." Why? Because we both said, "…For better or worse, for rich or for poor, in sickness and in health until death do us part." And we held on until we figured out how to navigate the falls.

Now, in the lap of calm waters, I can look back and say with satisfaction, "You DID remember to put the garbage cans out last night, didn't you?"(And not care so much if he didn't).

The Bible shouts warnings to any of us tempting to pull the plug on the marriage raft (the one posted below is written to men but applies to women equally). But success lies not in our ability but in God's capability. In every Extreme Sport of life, God is our Coach, our Belayer, our Guide, our All.

You cry out, "Why doesn't the LORD accept my worship?" I'll tell you why! Because the LORD witnessed the vows you and your wife made when you were young. But you have been unfaithful to her, though she remained your faithful partner, the wife of your marriage vows. Didn't the LORD make you one with your wife? In body and in spirit you are his… So guard your heart; remain loyal to the wife of your youth. "For I hate divorce!" says the LORD…To divorce your wife is to overwhelm her with cruelty, says the LORD of Heaven's Armies. so guard your heart; and do not be unfaithful to your wife. You have wearied the LORD with your words. "How have we wearied him?' you ask. You have wearied him by saying that all who do evil are good in the LORD'S sight, and he is pleased with them. You have wearied him
by asking, "Where is the God of justice?"
from Malachi 2:14-17

So again I say, each man must love his wife as he loves himself, and the wife must respect her husband.
Ephesians 5:33

72

Well, That's Sick

Inspired by our growing family, I started each day hugging the toilet. One pragmatic pre-teen would stand at the bathroom door holding their nose and shout over the heaving, "Hey Mom—should I make us eggs for breakfast?" To which I would immediately respond in the affirmative with another lunge into the commode. Morning sickness is considered a sign that the placenta is developing well, and reminding myself of that gave rise to "groanings to deep for words" and a final heave. I didn't love that.

Flu was another story. On rare occasions when I woke with a fever, my husband John, filled with sympathy (and eyeing eight hungry kids and not knowing where I kept—for example—the refrigerator), would pull from his pocket the tiny vial of anointing oil he keeps at the ready and offer the "fervent prayer of a righteous man." I prayed silently with him, "God, please ignore that prayer. I don't wanna be well. I wanna stay in bed a few days, serenaded by the children incessantly calling for "Dad" instead of "Mom." Sadly, I have a robust immune system.

In John 5:6, Jesus asked a paralyzed man, "Do you want to be made well?" What an odd question. I guess Jesus had seen the likes of me before. The paralytic doesn't answer

"Yes, Lord!" Instead, he states why he can't be well: he has no one to help him, others are in his way, yadayadayada.

In a spiritual sense, I sometimes feel paralyzed to walk God's path, to obey Him in the hard things He asks of me. There are perks to being unwell. I can be the victim; I can play the blame game. Being whole costs. I'll have to find new friends because all my supportive co-dependents won't want to play with me anymore. They may even try to sabotage my wellness. And, I'll need to take responsibility for myself: Get a grip, get a job, get a life…

Jesus breezes right past the excuses and tells the paralytic, "Get up…" Then, "Pick up your mat and walk." And, "Immediately the man was healed and he picked up his mat and walked."

I'm learning to just take the first step, to do the very next thing I know to do. Sometimes I expect voodoo, but the Lord says, "YOU do." We obey first, then He works the miracle.

Jesus has given us everything we need for life and godliness, so no matter what path He's chosen for us, we can get up, make our bed, and walk on. And, when rest is needed, He makes us lie down in green pastures—or cozy beds.

When Jesus saw him and knew he had been ill a long time, he asked him, "Would you like to get well?" "I can't, sir," the sick man said, "for I have no one to put me in the pool when the water bubbles up. Someone else always gets there ahead of me." Jesus told him, "Stand up, pick up your mat, and walk!"

John 5:6-8

By his divine power, God has given us everything we need for living a godly life…

2 Peter 1:3

73

OBEDIENCE OBSERVED

While walking in the park sans toilet seat cover (you'll know if you've read this book in order), I watched a little boy run toward the amusement rides across the street. As he approached the curb, his father commanded him to return. The little guy turned around, pleading for permission, but his father said firmly, "No, come here." The boy began to cry, not a tantrum-throwing cry, but sorrowful tears as he returned to his father, who sat with a baby on his lap. The boy hugged his father's leg, head resting on his knees, as his father tenderly stroked his hair.

This was not the slothful, idle-threat parenting nor the harsh, intolerant variety. Obviously, the father had invested in training his son for such a time when obedience could be a matter of life or death--which is the ultimate purpose of discipline, as stated in Proverbs 19:18, "Discipline your children, for in that there is hope; do not be a willing party to their death."

I was moved by this father's example of Ephesians 6:4, exhorting dads (likewise moms) to love and train their children: "Fathers, do not provoke your children to anger by the way you treat them. Rather, bring them up with the discipline and instruction that comes from the Lord."

Provocation results from the parenting pendulum stuck at either end: inconsistent rules and consequences at one or harsh, insensitive treatment at the other.

Bring them up means to nourish, nurture, and cherish them.

Discipline means cultivating their mind and morals through commands and rebuke (an abhorrent idea today—yet there it is).

Instruction connects our training of them to the Word of God. In other words, this kind of relationship is an enormous investment.

And that's parenting.

I had to remind myself of this when, while nursing a baby, the kids exploited my vulnerable position by sneaking off with forbidden fruit or, more likely, forbidden Legos before chores were done. Foremost in my thoughts—as I lugged my body off the couch, detached the (now crying) baby, chased down the culprit, and enforced the law—had to be,
"Eight kids? Am I crazy, or WHAT??!!? But that's another story.

The dad and son at the park also exemplify our Father's love for us and our response to His love. Like the little guy, I see the attractions and want what others are allowed to enjoy. My Father, knowing the perils, commands me to turn back. I feel frustrated, maybe even angry at God for not giving me what I need (from my near-sighted view). God does not jerk my arm, dragging me to His will. But He calls, and I hear Him. Like the dad at the park, the Lord allows emotional responses to His governance. He comforts us in the suffering that comes with obedience.

This relationship we have with our Father-- it's like a walk in the park.

This parenting relationship with our children is also a walk in the park...barefoot, over tiny sharp rocks. And hot coals. But in teaching them, we too, learn obedience.

For the Lord corrects those He loves, just as a father corrects a child in whom he delights.
Proverbs 3:12

Even though Jesus was God's Son, he learned obedience from the things he suffered.
Hebrews 5:8

...Your job is to obey the law, not to judge whether it applies to you.
James 4:11

74

GAMES I PLAY

I'm playing the old Whack-a-Mole game at the arcade in my head. Fear pops up, smack! Down it goes, but up pops anger, *BONK!* It disappears, but from the corner pops doubt. This happens when I try to handle things on my own—things like worry, resentment, and doubt. I may manage to beat down initial responses, but up pop more toothy heads with surprising force where least expected. I usually go a few rounds before realizing I'm in the game. And with this realization comes (eventually) handing the mallet to the only One who can win at this stuff.

When Jesus steps in, lights flash GAME OVER, clamoring bells and whistles halt, and things calm down, wa-a-y down. Then I tell Him that I haven't the slightest idea what I'm doing or how I'd do it even if I knew what I was doing…

"…I thought I was…"

"…But then they…"

"…so then I…"

"…it looks like…"

"…now I can't…"

And get this: He knows exactly what I'm talking about. He understands without sighing, "Haven't we been over this before?" Even though the answer is, "Yes, we have. Many times."

Together, we make an itemized list of what's really bugging me, and He only interrupts to say things like: "Umm…are you sure you want to defend yourself on this point? Shall I replay that particular portion of your life so you can see how it really went down?" Hint: Take His word for it. He's always right; just accept it. After all, to confess actually means to agree with. So do it. He knows what's what. Take His Word for it. Take His Word and apply it to every worry, angst, and doubt.

Here's how: Find a good Bible app for your phone, like Olive Tree or Blue Letter Bible. Look up the word *worry* (or fear or unbelief). For you newbies, find a translation you can actually comprehend, like the New Living Translation (NLT). And to you King James Only types, I say c'mon— when was the last time you heard someone say, "…So… we trussed up our fardels…" (A word my boys would add to their list of uproariously funny things to NOT SAY in front of Mom.) Okay, that's actually Acts 21:15 from the Geneva Bible, not King James, but still…

Then, scroll down the list of verses containing the word "worry" until you find verses to use as mallets the next time a mole rears its ugly head. Apply as needed. That's how to beat the game—any game— your mind invites you to play.

❋―――――――――――――❋

…We take every thought captive
to make it obedient to Christ.
2 Corinthians 10:5 NIV

…But the Son of God came to destroy
the works of the devil.
1 John 3:8

75

Now You Tell Me

I imagine the walls of hell plastered with this graffiti: IF ONLY…

Souls attempting to lie down and rest will be tormented by all the should've/could've/would'ves, i.e., regrets of this life. "If only I had chosen…" "If only I hadn't…"
I sometimes find myself experiencing a little bit of hell right here on Earth. I should've been a better mother/wife/Christian/teacher/cook/Scrabble player…ad infinitum.

A young woman haunted by guilt and regret once said, "I made such stupid choices, and now I'll never be able to live in the perfect will of God." I asked her two questions:

"Do you love God today?"

"Yes."

"Are you willing to do the very next thing He tells you to do?"

"Yes."

"Then you are in His perfect will."

God's grace works backward as well as forward. And, like syrup over waffles, his mercy fills every high and low place and every hole in between if we say "Yes" to Him right now.
So the next time the devil jabs you with his pitch-fork of "If Only…" snatch it from him and use it to roast marshmallows

at the campfire of the One who says, ALL THINGS work together for good, to those who love God and are called according to His purposes.

Regardless of your yesterday, NOW is the day of His grace; NOW is the day of salvation.

Who then is the one who condemns? No one.
Christ Jesus who died—more than that, who was
raised to life—is at the right hand of God
and is also praying for us.
Romans 8:34

If our hearts condemn us, we know that God is greater
than our hearts, and he knows everything.
1 John 3:20 NIV

76

CONFESSIONS OF A WIMPY PRAY-ER

If God does all things well, why am I always telling Him what to do? If He knows all things, why do I corner Him like a bore at a party with tedious information? Well, the thing is, He doesn't seem to mind. Case in point: Psalms. I guess being happy to hear from us, God takes what He can get; still, I'll try to tone it down a bit.

Andrew Murray wrote a book, *With Christ in the School of Prayer*. I'm waiting for the prequel: *With Christ in the Preschool of Prayer*. I have so much to learn. I do, however, have the User's Guide for prayer; it's called The Bible.

I used to think of prayer as nickels in a slot machine: Put in the prayer and pull the handle; oh shoot— two lemons and a cherry; no win this time. Put in another nickel…try again. But not one of our prayers is lost on God. Answers to our "dormant" prayers will come forth at the appointed time. He credits all my prayers to that day, that nano-second, when in "Thy will be done," He shouts, "Come Forth!" "Be Quiet!" "Come Out!" "Get up!" "Silence!" "Be still!"
Each phrase followed by "And suddenly…" It. Was. So. (John 11:43 NIV, Luke 4:35, Matthew 17:7, Mark 4:39.)

I do not need to know details in order to pray. I'm just to obey the Lord, who tells me to "watch and pray," "pray always," and "pray and not faint." To faint means to be spiritless, depressed, hopeless, or despondent. I am not to pray with a "what's the use" attitude, but with thanksgiving and trust—not in a guarantee I'll get what I want, but trust that *getting what God wants* is always best because He knows what I can't possibly know. My drone of knowledge is infinitesimal compared to Heaven's Satellite.

Our "canon of prayer" is a cannon of weaponry—not a drippy little squirt gun, but a missile hitting spot-on, tearing down strongholds, blowing doors wide open, disintegrating Satan's grip, and destroying our wrong thinking (2 Corinthians 10:3-5).

We persevere in perpetual petition with purposeful, powerful, and appreciative prayer (taken from Ephesians 6:18). Just saying that gets our lips moving in the right direction. And, we are to pray without ceasing, which means "without intermission." Intercession without intermission.

Until all hell breaks loose.

> Don't worry about anything; instead, pray about everything. Tell God what you need, and thank him for all he has done.
> Philippians 4:6

You are to name him Ishmael (which means 'God hears'), for the LORD has heard your cry of distress.
Genesis 16:11

The LORD hears the cry of the needy; he does not despise his imprisoned people.
Psalm 69:33

77

THE UNGODLY COUNCIL

My brain is hosting the Council of ungodly nations this morning. In the kitchen, my coffeemaker and I were minding our own business when suddenly, into the gray matter they marched, taking their seats and beginning their final argument with an itemized list of my criminal acts. Like I said, I was with the French press, who heard it all. Wow. What a list. I deserve a life sentence without parole. Move over, Paul; I'm the new C.O.S. (Chief of Sinners).

So, I do the only "think" I know to do. I plead guilty. "Yes. I know. I did that. And that, too. Yes, you're right; I have no basis for calling myself a Christian. Yes, yes, I'm a hypocrite and a real jerk, and I remember vividly what I did in 1983..."

Agreeing saves so much time. Attempting to parcel out, justify, or prove extenuating circumstances merely prolongs the trial. The Father of Lies tells the truth about my sins. But- regarding his recommendation of the eternal death penalty- he gravely errs.

The final blow of the gavel nailing Jesus to the cross, struck the Judge's stand, pardoning my criminal record: IT IS FINISHED.

Psalm 43 says, "Vindicate me, O God, and plead my cause against an ungodly nation; rescue me from deceitful and wicked men."

He did.

So now we'll enjoy a morning cup of coffee together.

And now, dear brothers and sisters, one final thing. Fix your thoughts on what is true, and honorable, and right, and pure, and lovely, and admirable. Think about things that are excellent and worthy of praise.
Philippians 4:8

Who will then condemn us? No one—for Christ Jesus died for us and was raised to life for us, and he is sitting in the place of honor at God's right hand, pleading for us.
Romans 8:34

3-Cord Wresting Match

The hardest part of our recent move was at the very end: wrestling the alligator. Okay, it was actually a queen-size 4" memory foam mattress we attempted to cajole into a large plastic bag. It thrashed—and thrashed us—before all was done.

We had a plan: I'd lay on top, pressing the air out as John followed close behind, rolling-squeezing-rolling the thing like one would if making a one-size-feeds-all Pigs-in-a-Blanket (lucky for John, that's my analogy, not his). All the while, John's knees scream at him from the hard floor, "We're too old for this!"

While John tended his knees, I quickly tackled the roll but bounced off. Unabashed—well, maybe a little bashed, we started again and decided tape was the answer.

John: "Where's the packing tape?"

Me: "Well, it's-uh, packed. But I'll find it."

We exchange places, limbs crisscrossing like wrestlers or a game of Twister without the dots, hampered by howling laughter as we considered what we'd look like on video… Thank God our kids are grown.

After rummaging through stacked-to-the-ceiling boxes in the car, I ran back upstairs, tape in hand. John held the foam seam tightly while I pulled the tape—all two inches of what remained on the dispenser.

Eventually, thanks to four black trash bags, six rubber bands, and a queen-size sheet, we wrestled what appeared to be a giant sushi roll out the door.

As we sat sweating on the porch steps, I was reminded of this verse: "Two people are better than one, for they can help each other succeed. A person standing alone can be attacked and defeated, but two can stand back-to-back and conquer. Three are even better, for a triple-braided cord is not easily broken" (Ecclesiastes 4:9,12).

Neither of us could have accomplished the task alone. One of the blessings (and challenges) of marriage is learning to work together, completing each other rather than competing. God puts opposites together for a reason; two opposite halves make a whole.

Beyond marriage, God has created in each of us a need for community. We are called to help and receive help, work together, be team players, and serve the Body of Christ in our church. This includes wrestling together through difficulties and differences.

Whether in marriage or in the fellowship of believers, recognizing Christ as the Overseer of every task gives strength, creativity, and wisdom beyond human capacity. Don't wrestle alone.

LIFE HACK: If you ever buy a large memory foam mattress topper, just leave it in its original bag until your final resting place. You'll thank me when it's time to move.

Or call us—we know what to do now: hire some young alligator wrestlers.

If one person falls, the other can reach out and help.
But someone who falls alone is in real trouble.
Ecclesiastes 4:10

A spiritual gift is given to each of
us so we can help each other.
1 Corinthians 12:7

Encourage each other and build each other up,
just as you are already doing.
1 Thessalonians 5:11

79

Love Your Crazy Neighbor as You Love Your Crazy Self

The Lord keeps things simple: Love God and love your neighbor. The problem is, my neighbors don't love me. Yet if I don't love my neighbor, I don't love God either, according to 1st John 4:20.

Biblically speaking, my neighbors are pure joy... "Consider it pure joy when you encounter trials of various kinds" (James 1:2).

Also, Jesus calls me to die to myself, and my neighbors lend a hand with that. But when I'm not busy dying, I stay out of their way.

One day, I realized how unhappy I must make them. I mean, they don't know Jesus, so this neighborhood is the closest thing they have to heaven, and we've sort of ruined that for them by living on land they consider their own (though it isn't).

I studied their lives and saw they were like the guy in the Bible who had been stripped, beaten, and left for dead (life does that, y'know). They needed first aid, a healing balm— the balm of kindness for starters, which our Great Physician so generously provides.

The pie chart of my life is covered in grace, yet, like an unmerciful servant, I dole out minuscule slivers according to what I think others deserve. Which is the direct opposite of grace; grace being undeserved blessing, and God says I owe them:

"Let no debt remain outstanding, except to love one another; for he who loves his neighbor has fulfilled the law" (Romans 13:8 NET).

God doesn't ask me to heal but to feel- to have compassion on those who press for control in an out-of-control world.

It's been a long and winding road with these neighbors- including a trip to the city council. I'd like to say things got better, but our judicial "win" lit a match under one female firecracker, prompting her to grab the face of another neighbor after the meeting.

"There's only one recourse..." said the Lord, "Invite her to lunch." Here's the unabridged version of that conversation:

Me: "NO."

God: "Yes."

Me: "NO."

God: "She's a damaged soul. Treat her like an honored guest."

Me: "I can't."

God: ....(Deafening Silence)...................

Me: (Whimpering) "Okaaay…but Your job is to change my heart because this can't be duty-driven. Give me a glimpse into her soul so I can see what You see and love like You love."

So He did, and though I had to practically drag that woman to my house, she came, and—here's the crazy—she loved it. She thanked me.

We sold our house the following year, and while packing, two of our most "joyous" neighbors (see James 1:2 for a refresher) came to say goodbye. The first tearfully apologized on behalf of himself and the neighborhood for "causing so much trouble." The lunch lady hugged me long and hard and said, "Thank you for being… kind. You've taught us a lot. I think we can be good neighbors now."

Wow--THIS. This was the Lord's doing. We thanked our neighbors and moved on knowing God, who "began a good work, will carry it on to completion" (Philippians 1:6).

Lord, you went to the cross for those I cross the street to avoid. Forgive me and give me a heart that yields when You say, "Look after this one, and when I return I will reimburse you for any extra expense you may have" (Luke 10:35).

Do not seek revenge or bear a grudge...but love your neighbor as yourself. I am the LORD.
Leviticus 19:18

If you can help your neighbor now, don't say, "Come back tomorrow, and then I'll help you."
Proverbs 3:28

It is a sin to belittle one's neighbor; blessed are those who help the poor [wretched, afflicted].
Proverbs 14:21 –parenthesis mine.

80

OUR HUMAN CONDITION

If we learned from our mistakes, I'd be a genius by now. My only hope is to help someone else avoid the same ones. On those rare occasions when someone asks me for counsel on parenting, I get all excited, as that is a subject upon which I can expound. I can't tell them what to do, but I am uniquely qualified to tell them what *not* to do, as I have forty-some years of mistakes from which to draw.

Speaking of mistakes, isn't it weird that my children, despite living with an exemplary sinner such as myself, will most likely make the same mistakes? All my brilliant mom-isms like "Eat your spinach or you'll poke your brother's eye out" may have all been in vain.

This is our human condition. We all step off the same curb into the same mud puddle. If we didn't, we wouldn't need Jesus.

I had a dream some years ago of attempting to rescue my children from a pending disaster when a voice said, "STOP! You can not save them, and you'll die trying." I awoke, strangled in the twisted sheets of this horrible truth: I CAN NOT SAVE THEM.

Parents can be as addicted to their beloved addict as the addict is to drugs. Our drug of choice is FIX IT. Detangling ourselves from the false assumption that salvation is "me finding the secret rescue recipe" is the first step to breathing again.

The second step is a giant leap: To respect our children's right to exercise free will. To respect their right to UNFOLLOW God. YIKES!! God places such value on free will that He allows the unconscionable; if He didn't, we'd all smell like fried ham from the lightning bolts. If He respects their choices, so must I (which is not to be confused with condoning or enabling).

Oh, the glory of surrender! I can lavishly love them now that my hands and heart are freed.

The real shock isn't that some of us are not saved, but that some of us *are*! God is not surprised by our rejection of Him. He said, "Everything man thinks or imagines is bent on evil from childhood" (Genesis 8:21).

His mighty arm that saved me is not too short to save those who follow in my mistaken footsteps. I breathe easier these days.

You must love the LORD your God...Keep in mind I am not talking now to your children, who have never...seen his greatness and his strong hand and powerful arm. Your children didn't see how the LORD cared for you in the wilderness until you arrived here...But you have seen the LORD perform all these mighty deeds with your own eyes!

Deuteronomy 11:5,7
Listen! The LORD's arm is not too weak to save you,
nor is his ear to deaf to hear you call.
Isaiah 59:1

...For I will fight those who fight you,
and I will save your children.
Isaiah 49:25

81

Did You Say, "A Yam?"

God identifies as I AM. At God's command, Moses was to convince his people that God was speaking to and through him, conveying an outrageous plan. Moses had a list of excuses for why their response might be, "That crazy Moe is at it again." And with good reason. Moses's last attempt at "saving people" ended very badly with him fleeing for his life (Exodus 2:11-14).

But ever the "glass half-full" kinda God, He sends Moses off with this sure-fire proof: "I AM that I AM. Tell them I AM sent you." (Exodus 3:14). ...Well. That's helpful. And by "helpful," I mean weird. Perhaps Moses' audience—and we, have been tempted to respond,

"You am WHAT, exactly? I don't have time for this. I need help here..."

"I AM."

"...I need answers..."

"I AM."

"...No, I mean a REAL answer; like, to life, to the ultimate questions..."

"I AM."

"STOP SAYING THAT and DO SOMETHING?!"

"I AM."

"I'm dying here and I need to know what's next, what's true, what's real, the end-all REALITY."

"I AM."

"Oh. My. GOD!&?!*"

"I AM."

Today, are *you* struggling to find an answer?

"I AM."

He himself gives life and breath to everything,
and he satisfies every need.
Acts 17:25

I know that my Redeemer lives. And after my body
has decayed, I will see Him with my own eyes.
Job 19:25a, 26a, 27a.

82

MARRIAGE—WITH BENEFITS

John and I would have irreconcilable differences, if not for our Wonderful Counselor. We're about as opposite as two people can be, and this is not some accident; it's God's plan.

Our languages differ: John's love-language is verbal encouragement and physical affection. Okay, let's be honest —sex. Mine? Vacuum the floor, and I'm all over you. Well, not you—him (finish the vacuuming first, of course). I'm quick, he's thoughtful, I'm organized, he's a collector— as I write, I'm looking at his collection of socks on the floor. I see what is, he envisions what could be. I do my best thinking at five in the morning, he is most creative at night. In parenting, I'm the detective, he's the counselor. My idea of a vacation is to camp and hike, his is a stack of books beside an overstuffed chair next to a crackling fire (after eight kids, I admit his idea has more appeal). Early in our marriage, I freaked out if we didn't have money in savings while he played the ATM like an ever-winning slot machine, but he protected us from debt by avoiding credit cards.

This is just a sample of our differences. Pretty much, you name it, we're opposites. But we have some all-important similarities: Singularly and together, we have a non-negotiable love and commitment to Jesus. And, before we married, we decided divorce would be a four-letter word, never to be mentioned in our home—not verbally, not mentally. That and prayer kept us safe from our really wacky ideas about marriage, like, we thought it'd be okay to give each other privacy and respect if an old boyfriend/girlfriend showed up at the door—Yikes!! The Lord protected us and changed our minds right quick after the first ring of the doorbell.

So, how did we get here fifty years later? "Here" being very much in love, and each other's Favorite Everything.

We forgive a lot. We forget it, too—which has become easier as we've hit seventy-ish.

We cover each other's backs. We speak to each other in words and tone like we would a stranger at the grocery store, saying stuff like, "Thank you." "Excuse me." "Here—let me help you with that." We make adjustments and allowances. John leaves junk mail on the floor next to his chair; I put a trash basket right where he drops it. Ta-Da! Problem solved. I get twitchy about finances (or lack thereof); he takes over paying the bills.

This we know:
- We will not change each other. God may, but that's *His* business.
- We will both make big mistakes—how else do we learn?
- We will get through it.

Our business is to love each other deeply, pray for each other daily, and adjust, yield, serve, and bend—which are palatable ways of saying, "We die to ourselves." Is that a bad thing? In this day, it would seem so, but we are living proof that the outcome is being BLISSED and BLESSED. Of course, we wouldn't have that if we didn't believe in longevity and the utter, unfailing faithfulness of God.

Everything changes when we say "I Do" to Jesus Christ.

In his grace, God has given us different gifts for doing certain things well.
Romans 12:6

Love each other with genuine affection, and take delight in honoring each other.
Romans 12:10

Let each of you look not only to his own interests, but also to the interests of others.
Philippians 2:4 ESV

83

HULL OF FAITH

Recently, while nursing a bad attitude, I mouthed a prayer—a brief, half-hearted S.O.S. and to my surprise, a word popped into my head. The word was "barnacles." Huh. Kinda fishy. I've used that word maybe a total of zero times in my lifespan (not counting Scrabble games), so I did a bit of research and found this bit of information: The Navy estimates that barnacles on ships can increase weight and drag by 60% and fuel consumption by 40%.

As barnacles grow on ships, I allow similar drags to affix themselves to my faith in Christ. Has some invasive entity attached itself to the bottom line of, "For by grace you have been saved through faith, not by works…?"

I'm not referring to giant crustaceans of sin. Walking with Christ daily, we generally keep our scraper handy for those. I'm addressing the smaller species of self-made rules and regulations and overweening duties that latch on and erode our hull of faith, producing a bogged-down attitude toward our Christian walk and, ultimately, a secret cynicism toward God Himself. In essence, we become crabby in faith. While "faith without works is dead," faith REPLACED by work is also death. Jesus never intended us to sail the seas of life apart from His fuel—His power—flowing through us.

Jesus says, "Come to me...Let me teach you. Because I am humble and gentle at heart and you will find rest for your souls. For my yoke is easy to bear, and the burden I give you is light" (Matt. 11:29-30).

"Humble and gentle" is pretty much what I'm not (refer to "bad attitude" above). Only as I return to the ship—the relationship with Jesus Christ—and let the waves of His nature wash over me, can I set sail on a new course, one where duty is steered by the rudder of faith. Then it'll be free-sailing as I run in the paths of His commands.

Let me ask you this one question: Did you receive the Holy Spirit by obeying the law...? Of course not! You received the Spirit because you believed the message you heard about Christ. How foolish can you be? After starting your new lives in the Spirit, why are you now trying to become perfect by your own human effort?

Galatians 3:2,3

84

They Are Us

If you are disgusted and discouraged by the hypocrisy of church leaders, you are closer to Christ than you think. Jesus saved His harshest words for those who claimed to represent God but whose words didn't match their actions. He wasn't afraid to call them out, using choice names like "venomous snakes" and "white-washed tombs." He also took a whip and caused a considerable disturbance at the worship center.

So don't let others' hypocrisy—or your own (C'mon—Your words don't always match your actions), keep you from Jesus or His church.

Jesus is who He says, does what He promises, and never changes. And despite the occasional snake at the altar and wolf in the pew, Jesus still chose the temple as a platform for His messages. He'll deal with the snakes and wolves. He knows how to clean house.

I read in Matthew chapter 23 how Jesus handled hypocrisy. But just as I'm cheering, "Get 'em, God!" I recall Romans 3:10, which speaks of my own wicked little heart:

"There is NONE who does good," —and in case I beg to differ, He adds— "No—not one."

It's why He came.

And let us not neglect our meeting together, as some people do, but encourage one another, especially now that the day of his return is drawing near.
Hebrews 10:25

They worshiped together at the Temple each day, met in homes for the Lord's Supper, and shared their meals with great joy and generosity.
Acts 2:46

[Anna]…never left the Temple but stayed there day and night, worshiping God with fasting and prayer.
Luke 2:37

85

MINE YOURS

"It's a waste of time and money; that dirt is ninety-eight percent waste material." But the young entrepreneur had his eyes on that other two percent, so ignoring the naysayers, Daniel Cowan Jackling began mining, and persistence paid off. Since the meager beginning, more precious minerals have been extracted than the combined value of the Comstock, Klondike, and the California Gold Rush.

There's a correlation between mining and reading the Bible. I'm reminded of my first years as a new follower of Jesus. I'd heard of the promised "victorious life" but wondered how in the world to get from here to there. *Here* being the swarming fruit flies of sin reproducing in me (and bugging anyone who came near). I observed the character qualities of mature believers—those who bore fruit minus the flies—and noted a common trait: They loved God's Word, and dedicated themselves to studying it.

So, I decided to read the Bible every day. Initially, I didn't comprehend much of it (think two percent). But as I persisted in "mining the gold," I determined not to concern myself with what I didn't understand, but act on the small percentage I did, and ask God about the rest (especially stuff I didn't like). I attended a church that taught through the Bible, verse by verse, filling many gaps. Of course, I don't understand everything; some things can't be known this side of heaven.

Just as Jackling developed tools to increase productivity, I, too, implement helps:

• First, I expect God to speak to me through His Spirit because He said He would (John 15:15, Psalm 25:14,15, Jeremiah 33:3, Job 33:14-18, John 10:27-28). Perhaps not immediately, but like a slow-release vitamin, the Word penetrates mind and soul.

• Second, I ask myself three questions,

What does it say?

What does it mean?

What does it mean to ME?"

These suggestions and more can be found on Anne Graham Lotts' website, AnGeL Ministries.

• Third, I write down my observations in a prayer form, beginning with thanks for whatever (there are plenty of "whatevers" even on the worst days) and asking the Lord to help me with the next step, which is...

• Fourth, DO IT.

I recommend starting with an easy-to-read translation unless you commonly text friends with things like, "Refresh my bowels in the Lord." (Philemon 1:20, King James Version). Find an ESV or NLT (the NLT has an excellent New Believer's Bible with helpful notes).

Start with the words of Jesus—one of the four gospels—and don't go all OCD on formulas, tools, or missing a day. Slip-ups happen. This is mining, not ice-climbing.
In mining the Word, I've hit the Mother Lode of abundant life: every spiritual blessing Jesus promised; "everything we need for life and godly living" (2 Peter 1:3).

When it comes to treasure, make mine the Bible.

They searched the Scriptures day after day to see if Paul and Silas were teaching the truth.
Acts 17:11

...To make her holy and clean, washed by the cleansing of God's word.
Ephesians 5:26

I rejoice in your word like one who discovers a great treasure.
Psalm 119:162

86

I Hear Ya (Weh)

In the seventh and eighth months of gestation, an infant's heart rate slows down slightly whenever his/her mother speaks, indicating the calming effect of the mother's voice, and at birth, can identify her voice apart from others, due to the relationship developed between the one who provides everything necessary for life (the mother) and the receiver (the baby).

I started thinking about this in light of how the Lord speaks to us. Though rarely audible, He does speak nonetheless—directly, intimately, frequently, when least expected and most needed, as we stay close and dependent through prayer, reading His Word, and —most importantly, as we trust Him and obey. In fact, the only time God doesn't speak is when I've ignored the last thing He told me to do, or I'm so full of my own voices He can't get a word in edgewise (pride, fear, and bitterness being the biggest loudmouths). But He'll try again when the line isn't busy.

Knowing He speaks to me is an inexpressible comfort. For instance, I lay in bed this morning suffering from fleas—those small, biting "if only I'd..." regrets. When that voice, so contrary to my own in its confident and lighthearted bent broke in: "Yeah, yeah, and THAT'S why you need a Savior..."

To which I responded, "Oh—Right."

Most treasured is this aspect of our relationship. Jesus treats me like a friend, a daughter, and a bride, not because I'm anything special, but because He is.

Do you know His voice? If not, ask Him to speak to you, like Samuel did: "Speak, Lord, Your servant is listening." Keep asking and keep listening. The first thing out of His mouth may be something hard to swallow, like, "I love you."

Believing that is the start of an ongoing, life-long conversation. And, like a baby soothed by the mother's voice, your heart rate will slow with the calming effect of knowing He "joys over you with singing."

> The Lord your God is living among you. He is a mighty Savior. He will take delight in you with gladness. With His love, He will calm all your fears. He will rejoice over you with joyful songs.
> Zephaniah 3:17

> [Jesus said] "I tell you, keep on asking...keep on seeking...keep on knocking...For everyone who asks, receives. Everyone who seeks, finds. And to everyone who knocks, the door will be opened."
> Luke 11:9, 10

87

Fully Charged

Ten girlfriends were on a tour bus headed for New York to Times Square for the big New Year's Eve Party at the Renaissance Hotel. With tickets bought and safely stored in their phones, the girls spent the day laughing, chatting, and taking group selfies in anticipation of this once-in-a-lifetime event. Five girls had the forethought to fully charge their phones; the other five did not. Traffic was horrid, and the girls whose phones had not been charged began flashing "low battery" signals in the unexpected delay. Panicked, they asked to borrow their friends' phones, but of course, that would not get them into the event. By the time they arrived in New York City, five girls were out of power, and all the Apple stores were closed. Tragically, only the five girlfriends who'd powered up got in.

I call this my parable of the ten girlfriends.

The Bible warns us of much more significant loss and consequences in the parable of the ten virgins (Matthew 25:1-13), yet the points to ponder are similar:

We are all on this faith journey together, yet when tragedy strikes, we will individually stand or fall according to the source of our strength. While friends and family are a great comfort, they can not transfer their faith to us in our time of need. We must be personally connected, not just on an occasional plug-in basis, but on a continuous feed, to the Power that will sustain us in this life and the next. Jesus offers to take care of us in every way because He IS the Way —the Cord and the Power—technologically speaking, by which we have access to all the resources we need.

His divine power has given us everything we need for life and godliness through getting to know, personally and intimately, the One who invited us to God.
2 Peter 1:3

The kingdom of God is not just a lot of talk;
it is living by God's power.
1 Corinthians. 4:20

88

OPEN INVITATION

While wrestling a straw through the foil hole in a juice pack for the grandkids, I squirted the counter, floor, and them with sticky wetness and muttered to no one in particular, "In my day, we just drank from the carton."

Everything takes some sort of tool to open these days. Toys used to come in a box. Now, the packaging is simply a cover for a diabolical plot enticing grandma to say a naughty thing in front of her grandchildren as she tries to clip the twenty wires that hold the doll, the truck, or the pajamas onto the cardboard backing. HECK AND THE DEVIL!

And don't even get me started on the clamshell cases for batteries, electronic gadgets, and—I predict eventually—toilet paper. It's all so overwhelming I have a headache. But I can't get the lid off the pain meds.

All this got me thinking...some people complain about Jesus's claim to be the only way to God. "So narrow," they say. And Jesus would agree. It is the narrow way. Very, very, narrow. It's kind of like gate B-5 at the airport terminal. But I look around and don't hear anyone balking at the airline's narrowness of insisting we go through that particular gate to reach our destination.

So yeah—it's narrow, but He is also the OPEN way. No wrestling with self-righteous packaging, no twisting ties of dogma to unravel or cut through, no plastic sealant or wad of white fluff the size of a small cotton field to keep us from His comforting presence.

Just walk on through, to life.

> Jesus said, "Yes, I am the gate. Those who come in through me will be saved."
> John 10:9

> And, "I have set before you an open door..."
> Revelation 3:7

89

GREAT EXPECTATIONS

Expectations. My sister Peggy calls them "planned disappointments." We all have a chronic case of them, which is why Jesus said in Matthew 11:6, "Blessed are those who do not fall away on account of Me." This was a heads-up that life and God do not do our bidding. Yet, aren't we astonished when reality bulldozes our expectations? Which I calculate to be approximately 102% of life.

For newlyweds, it's the discovery that he drinks from the carton and belches from his inmost being and that she is hormonally schizophrenic fourteen days out of every month, or thirteen if he's lucky. For most of us, expectations are dreams turned nightmares.

Whether it's a slow dawning or a quick jolt slapping us out of our la-la land, there's a suffering to bear in unmet expectations, and as in any grief, there's a pattern (usually) and a process (always).

My first drug of choice in coping with life's disappointments is denial, though it's the first yellow brick on the road to insanity. Depending on our coping skills and creativity, there is no end to the lengths we'll go as we attempt to keep reality from popping out of the box, Jack, but words like "obsessive," "excessive," and "destructive" are usually involved. Denial forces the creation of clever diversion tactics for some, and for others, ABSOLUT ®ly.

The alternative? Acknowledgment, but that takes courage. It says, "This thing (guilt, grief, disappointment) is alive, and it's not going away," which is the first step toward holding a memorial service and scattering the ashes of our beloved expectation. That's not a bad thing, though tears aren't easily convinced. It often takes the death of something to open our closed minds to new ideas and our eyes to the truth.

The Bible tells us it took the death of Isaiah's close relationship with Uzziah to open his eyes to something— someone— greater: "In the year King Uzziah died, I saw the Lord, seated on His throne...." (Isaiah 6:1). This revelation led to new adventures for Isaiah and a closer relationship with the King of Kings.

Reality is not what I expected. I thought coming to Christ was my free ticket to Happily Ever After. To which Jesus says, "Well yes, but...you have to die first."
It's in that surrender I find something better than happy. I find unexpected joy, unswayed by circumstance.

I often ask myself, What did you *expect*? Give it up. Give it over to the Lover of your Soul. Whether it be shattered dreams or a broken heart, face this death. Face it, facing Him. Face Him wearing your angry eyes if that's the reality. Maybe it'll help a little to know He cries, too.

Life can be emotionally abusive. Reality is truth. Truth hurts, but then it sets you free. So, walk in truth. Or crawl, if necessary. And you can expect, without disappointment, that Christ walks with you.

> If you continue in my word, you are really my
> disciples, and you will know the truth,
> and the truth will set you free.
> John 8:11,12

> In the year King Uzziah died, I saw the Lord,
> seated on His throne, high and exalted
> Isaiah 6:1

90

That Rocka'Feller

John Rockefeller became wealthy by reading the Bible and believing it. He read Genesis 11:3, which is the story of The Tower of Babel and a description of the advanced technology of the inhabitants of Shinar:

"They had brick for stone and asphalt for mortar."

Rockefeller figured where there was asphalt, there must be oil, so the Standard Oil company began the exploration of oil deposits in Iraq. And the rest is history.

What if I lived believing that every fact in the Bible was true? What if I lived according to everything I've read about the love of God, the forgiveness in Jesus, and the power of the Holy Spirit? What would my life look like?

"The fool says in his heart, 'There is no God.'" (Ps. 14:1) Am I not that fool to settle for a life lived according to what I tell myself, my limited resources, and conjured assumptions rather than what God has said in His Word?

What if I lived like that Rocke-feller? Now THAT would be rich.

Every word of God proves true...
Proverbs 30:5

Don't just listen to the Word and deceive yourself.
Do what it says.
James 1:22

All scripture is God-breathed and is useful for teaching,
correcting, and training in right living, so that the
servant of God may be completely equipped
for every good work.
2 Timothy 3:16-17

91

Quirks of Art

My preschool students made construction paper ladybugs. I'd displayed a model to follow, placed the various pieces in small trays, and let them go at it. The end results made me smile all day.

One little guy decided the antennae made an excellent handlebar mustache. Another placed the wings upside-down so the bug looked like the top bird on a totem pole. A little girl discovered my sticker drawer and buried her bug under neon sticky dots. One pragmatic student simply stacked all the pieces in a pile and glued them. There. Done. To his thinking, time is much better spent engineering the latest Lego construct; all this gluing and arranging is nothin' but a bunch of craft.

But here's the thing: When displayed together on the wall, the motley crew of paper and glue look undeniably like what they were intended to be: ladybugs. A joyous, raucous exhibit of creativity and originality, but still linked to the model somehow.

Just like the people in our church. Jesus is our model (Ephesians 5:1,2), the Holy Spirit has imparted a variety of gifts (Hebrews 2:4), and we are God's work of art (Ephesians 2:8-10).

We are a joyous, creative, motley crew, and the thing is, when grouped together, we are undeniably what we are intended to be: The Body of Christ, bringing great joy to Him.

Beware that you don't look down on
any of these little ones...
Matthew 18:10

...Why do you look down on another believer?...
Romans 14:10

In his grace, God has given us different gifts
for doing certain things well...
Romans 12:6

92

Shelter in Place

A few years ago, while assisting a church, we experienced Hurricane Earl in Belize, Central America. Waiting for a hurricane to hit is like waiting in line to ride the exciting and white-knuckling rollercoaster at Disneyland, the one where everyone ends up drenched in water, except hurricanes are not tested for safety, and seat belts are not included.

We prepared by placing plywood over all the windows, dragging a rowboat up to the back porch, and, since we were caring for our friend's dogs, we gave them a life vest demonstration "in the unlikely event of a water landing."

The ocean was a sleeping sea monster, green and ominous in its stillness. We visited and revisited the beach to gaze at the water; sometimes, it just feels good to be scared. This was not one of those times.

Local T.V. stations listed various shelters in the area in case the big bad Earl threatened to huff and puff and blow the houses down, as hay and sticks (thatch and stilts) are common building materials in Belize.

Power to the town is turned off before a sizable storm hits, which is a bit unnerving when the storm is set to make landfall in the middle of the night. We understood if evacuation was necessary, our phone flashlights would be of little help, so John and I did what we knew to do: We ate all the ice cream in the freezer and went to bed.

We did, in fact, end up at a shelter, but not one recommended by local authorities. Our shelter is this one found in Psalm 91:1: "Those who dwell in the shelter of the Most High will rest in the shadow of the Almighty."

In the original language of the Old Testament, *dwell* means "to remain, to make one's home, to continue in." *Shelter* is "a secret place, a covering; a protected place." *Rest* means to "pass the night," and *shadow* is "the place of shade." *The Most High and Almighty* is the One who is "High and Mighty"— Higher and Mightier than whatever storm we face.

I go to this shelter often. In fact, I live there. It's an all-purpose shelter. Whether the storm is external or internal, circumstantial or relational. It's not a cement-cold cellar; it's the most soothing place on earth. It's my Happy Place.

So run and hide. Run to the LORD and hide in the shelter of His presence.

Guard me as you would guard your own eyes.
Hide me in the shadow of your wings.
Psalm 17:8

Be merciful to me, O God, be merciful to me!
For my soul trusts in You; And in the shadow of Your wings I will make my refuge, until these calamities have passed by.
Psalm 57:1

Show me the wonders of your great love,
you who save by your right hand those who take refuge in you from their foes.
Psalm 17:7

93

Traveling Companion

To really know someone, travel with them. You'll discover their raw essence—and yours, for better or worse. You may be relieved by your travel mate's ability to adapt in stressful situations or be amused to find a seemingly "go with the flow" personality becomes anything *but* when the "flow" is a public toilet in rural Asia. By public, I mean outside, and by toilet, I mean ditch. We may think we know someone, but the truth is, we won't really know them until we've traveled hard times together.

This is true of our relationship with the Lord. Job, the poster child for "Life is Bad and Then We Die," traveled the terrain of humiliation, loss, grief, and physical pain beyond imagination—I mean, really—*boils*? Was that necessary? I imagine the outbreak came right after Job looked around at the dung heap his life had become and said something like, "Well…at least I still have nice skin."

In the end, the story of Job plays like a country song, "…Got the wife back, the kids back, and the critters, too…" But more than the return of all his earthly rewards was this: Knowledge of the Holy One.

Do you want to know Christ, *really* know Him? The good news is this is God's will for you. The bad news is it comes through suffering. The great news is the intimacy found in the fellowship of suffering with Christ surpasses pain. Not many of us will suffer as Job did, thankfully, but with the sufferings we are given, will we allow the Lord to make Himself known to us? If so, we'll come through saying, "I knew *of* You, I knew *about* You, but now I *know You*."

It's comforting to travel with someone familiar with the territory, someone who won't "ditch" you. Jesus has traveled all regions of suffering, and He who traveled before us travels with us.

My ears had heard of you, but now
my eyes have seen you.
Job 42:5

For you have been given not only the privilege of trusting in Christ, but also the privilege of suffering for him.
Philippians 1:29

I want to know Christ and experience the mighty power that raised him from the dead. I want to suffer with him, sharing in his death.
Philippians 3:10

94

WORD.

It may be the most common natural disaster. It goes by many descriptive terms, such as: "I believe in speaking my mind." "I call it as I see it." "I'm just being honest."

I'm referring, of course, to our words—or, as the Bible calls it, "The Tongue."

I'm an authority on the subject because if my legs ran as fast as my mouth, I'd be an Olympic medalist. My husband John speaks fluent patience, So I sometimes ask myself, "What would John not say?" When I'm all done not saying anything, I need two aspirin and a bed. If only I could retain control as easily as I retain water.

I encourage John with, "Be glad I'm not a Lemur; they have two tongues."

I suspect the apostle Paul of struggling with his tongue, too: "...When I want to do what is right, I inevitably do what is wrong... Who will free me from this life dominated by sin and death?" But Paul gives me hope with his subsequent statements: "The answer is in Jesus Christ our Lord...And because you belong to him, the power of the Holy Spirit has freed you from the power of sin..." (from Romans chapters 7 and 8). There's hope for me!

I pray for the transforming power of the Holy Spirit and apologize for my unholy spirit. To speed the process along, I memorize Bible verses about the tongue. There are over a hundred, and clearly, the Lord sees control of the mouth as a matter of blessing or curse, life and death, and marriage or divorce.

The Bible says a tiny spark from our tongue can set a great forest on fire. So I'm just being honest, speaking my mind, and calling it as I see it when I look in the mirror and say to myself,

"Only YOU can prevent forest fires."

Set a guard, O Lord, over my mouth;
keep watch over the door of my lips.
Ps. 141:3

And the tongue is a flame of fire...It can set your whole
life on fire, for it is set on fire by hell itself.
James 3:6

A wise woman builds her house, but the foolish
woman plucks it down with her own hands.
Proverbs 14:1

95

He's Strong When I'm Meek

The narrow road has steep learning curves. As a new believer, I bristled at the Bible verses highlighting meekness as a virtue for followers of Christ. My M.O. was more freaked and riled than meek and mild. I considered meekness weakness. Did the Divine require me to de-spine?

Actually, meekness is restrained strength, exhibited especially in times of tremendous pressure. It resists the urge to hurt or control despite having the power or reason to do so. It's a German Shepherd allowing a toddler to jump on his neck, tug his ear, and pull his tail and nose. One snap of the mighty jaw could end it all, but he withholds his power, suffering the indignities, submitting to the little one for love's sake; that's meekness.

If I belong to Christ, I, too, must model this characteristic of speaking and acting with restraint, for nothing characterizes Christ more than meekness. One word from His bloodied mouth could have destroyed His enemies, but He restrained His power, suffered, and died to restore our friendship with God (Romans 5:10). Then He got up, brushed himself off, visited His friends, and sat down next to His Dad in Heaven. That's meekness: power controlled.

Meekness is neither resignation nor passive submission, though it may appear so to the clueless. The Greek word when referring to animals is "tame." Taming doesn't produce weakness but bridled strength. No longer a bucker-kicker-biter, the horse learns to work in unity with the one who holds the reins.

Lord, may I yield to Your reign so I can work in unity with You. As I learn meekness, maybe this ram of God can become more like the Lamb of God.

Though he [Jesus] was God, he did not think of equality with God as something to cling to. Instead, he gave up his divine privileges; he took the humble position of a slave...he humbled himself in obedience to God and died a criminal's death on a cross. Therefore, God elevated him to the place of highest honor.
Philippians 2:6-9

Since God chose you to be the holy people he loves, you must clothe yourselves with tenderhearted mercy, kindness, meekness, gentleness and patience making allowance for each other's faults and forgiving anyone who offends you. Remember the Lord forgave you, so you must forgive others.
Colossians 3:12

96

DRAW BRIDGE

I was helping with a garage sale when a man I recognized from around town came up to buy a few things. He's recognizable by his long gray beard, floral dresses, and a purse just like my grandma's. I was mentally twitchy and uncomfortable, so I decided to chat with him and found we had much in common—we'd lived in the same places and had mutual friends. I also noticed this man had gentle eyes, eyes softened by pain, and as I began to pray for him, I sensed the Lord helping me form a question I wanted to ask. I said,

"So…tell me a little about your fashion choices. I've seen you around town and wondered."

He said he was in a body cast his first twelve years, preventing him from wearing pants, so He wore skirts. His mother's boyfriends belittled him, and when the cast was finally removed, he wore pants but had trouble walking and fell into a creek at school one day. When he stumbled into class covered in mud, His teacher said,

"Well, if that's the best you can do in boy clothes, we'll dress you as a girl." She made him wear a dress, frilly socks, and a bow in his hair.

He told me he was taken to a psychiatrist as a teen. The psychiatrist told him to go downtown, find a prostitute, pay for her services, and he'd never want to dress like a woman again. He told the psychiatrist he didn't believe in sex before marriage, so he couldn't do that.

After serving in the army, he married and was married and had children. A divorce came eighteen years later. He's worked many years for the forestry service and oversaw the rebuilding of four churches in the south burned to the ground by the KKK. The only one he felt ever truly loved him was his mother. When she died, he began wearing her clothes. He told me that though he is not gay, the only people who welcome him are gay.

I listened and prayed and hugged him as He shared his story, and then I told Him about one of the names of God, El Roi, the "God who sees."

"God wants you to know He saw you in that body cast and all you suffered. He knows your pain. He loves you and desires to heal all the hurts from your past."

I invited him to church. He said he probably wouldn't be accepted there. I said, "Well, come sit by me."

Here's what I'm learning: There are reasons people are the way they are. We are all broken; we've all skewed what God designed. We are all poor and needy. But if I let go of my fears, God will give me a glimpse into people's souls, so I can address THAT rather than the surface things that make me so very uncomfortable. God helps us find a bridge—a common tie, to that one seemingly beyond our reach. God loves to do that; after all, He sent Jesus to be our High priest —our bridge—between God and us, and we are called to be bridges between Jesus and others.

He [Jesus] will not judge by appearances, nor make a decision based on hearsay; he will give justice to the poor, and make fair decisions for the exploited.*
Isaiah 11:3
*[exploited can be defined as "the weak, afflicted, miserable"]

...Yes, I try to find common ground with everyone, doing everything I can to save some.
1 Corinthians 9:22

97

FRIEND REQUEST

"I don't mean to hurt your feelings, but I don't believe in God," said my young friend as we visited via FaceTime.

"I went to church a few times with my cousin, and I liked it—I mean, the people were nice and everything, but then the priest or pastor or whatever said we had to love God more than anyone else, even our family. I just didn't think that was right, so I quit going."

"Well, that doesn't hurt my feelings," I assured, "And I understand your frustration. To be commanded to love a stranger would be awkward and even dangerous. We wouldn't friend someone on Facebook without checking them out. We'd get on their page, check their 'about' info, and see what they represent. We need to know who we're following. God said to love Him above everything and everyone else, but He wasn't speaking to strangers. He was speaking to His children. He proved His love for them by protecting, providing, guiding, and always keeping His promises, as good fathers do. His children had His very best love, and so it was fair to expect them to respond with their very best love."

I encouraged her to check Him out, to pray, asking God to make Himself known because He said, "When you look for me with all your heart, you will find me."

I, too, don't like some things Jesus says (He can be a real party pooper at my pity parties). I recall others who had the same problem in John chapter 6. It started so well. Jewish followers of Jesus had a political game plan. Their campaign slogan could've read:
JESUS FOR JEWS IN A.D. 32!

But then Jesus went rogue, saying, "Eat my flesh and drink my blood..." With that, popular opinion did an about-face. "King of the Jews" became "Crazy Cannibal Guy," and "...Many disciples deserted him." (John 6:66)

If they'd stuck around, they'd have learned that "eating and drinking" meant "believing and trusting" in his broken body, and "poured out blood" equaled a redemption far more significant than mere political buyback.

Jesus doesn't get hurt feelings (but He does anguish) when people reject Him. He knows most will. He uses the word "if" a lot: "'If' anyone wants to follow Me..." "'If' you love Me...." Jesus places enormous value on free choice (thus, bad things happen). We choose to love Him or choose to ignore Him. But His Friend Request still stands.

Look, I stand at the door and knock. IF you hear my voice and open the door, I will come in and we will share a meal together as friends.
Revelation 3:20

"But some of you don't believe me… That is why I said that people can't come to me unless the Father gives them to me." At this point many of his disciples turned away and deserted him.
John 6:66

98

TRANS-formed Mind

Perched on the kitchen counter while I tied his shoes, my four-year-old son stated matter-of-factly, "I wish I was a girl."

"You wish you were a GIRL? Why!?" I asked.

"I wish I was a girl 'cuz I don't like myself."

"Well..." praying to respond aptly, "I love you *and* I like you." I went on, listing the things I loved about him, but I knew it wasn't enough.

This child, sandwiched between two siblings who'd cornered the market on validation through their skills and/or sheer cuteness, struggled for attention. He'd establish himself in a tigger sort of way—bouncy and flouncy, rather like a three-ring circus unto himself.

I shared this conversation with John, and after praying and letting the dust settle, we knew we had to act. Our hearts ached for him, and we asked the Lord to give us wisdom in helping our son find that "buried treasure"—the gifts and talents God had created in him—shrouded by insecurity.

We removed stressors (piano lessons) that fed unhealthy competition, focused on helping him succeed in new areas (guitar), catered schooling to his learning style (kinesthetic) and created avenues for his gifts to be displayed and appreciated by others. Over time, self-confidence increased, and leadership skills matured as certain as his manhood.

Children are vulnerable to chaotic thinking. (Aren't we all?) The solution lies not in changing what God designed them to be but in nurturing a love for what God designed them to be. As they learn to know, love, and respect Him, they will know, love, and respect themselves. There is no peace apart from this—all else is chaos.

Let's teach our children well-ness, along with shoe-tying.

> When I was a child, I spoke and thought and reasoned as a child. But when I grew up, I put away childish things. Now we see things imperfectly, like puzzling reflections in a mirror, but then we will see everything with perfect clarity. All that I know now is partial and incomplete, but then I will know everything completely, just as God now knows me completely.
> 1Corinthians 13:11,12

> You made all the delicate, inner parts of my body and knit me together in my mother's womb. Thank you for making me so wonderfully complex! Your workmanship is marvelous—how well I know it.
> Psalm 139:13,14

99

NEW MATH

The hardest part of forgiving others is doing the math. Peter came to Jesus and asked, "Lord, how often should I forgive someone who sins against me? Seven times?" Jesus replied, No, not seven times, but seventy times seven" (Mt. 18:21,22).

An equally challenging equation is found in the Lord's Prayer: "Forgive us our trespasses as we forgive those who trespass against us."

Which looks like this:
GFM=T°IWIFO=(God forgives me equal to the degree in which I forgive others).

I prefer something simple like I=I, "An eye for an eye." But Jesus did away with old math (Matthew 5:38-47). And who am I kidding? I only like that equation if I'm not the "eye" involved.

"Hate math," my eye.

The real problem lies in subtraction: I don't want anyone to take away my right to resentment and self-pity. In addition, I calculate the precise amount of mercy owed, and not a fraction more, like Scrooge bent over his accounts on Christmas Day.

Enter Jesus, who took all my calculations to the cross and stamped, "Paid in Full" with only 1 requirement: Receive His forgiveness and pass it on.
Problem solved.

For Your honor O LORD, forgive my many, many sins.
Psalm 25:11

Then Jesus said to the woman, Your sins are forgiven.
Luke 7:48

Wisdom will multiply your days
and add years to your life.
Proverbs 11:9

100

We're Expecting

We're excited: Today is our maiden voyage with our new TSA PreCheck status.

Except, it isn't.

Upon showing our passports, John and I were chosen for a random search. Two agents lead us off our yellow brick road to the table and hand-held scanners.

"But...we're TSA Pre..." I whimper as I remove my backpack.

"Oh, don't worry, you'll be through before anyone else in this line," said the agent.

Except we aren't.

Well, I mean, John gets an A+ despite carrying a truckload of tech equipment, batteries, chargers, earphones, modems, microchips and dip, and-who-knows-what-all. But not only do I NOT get TSA PRE; I get ANTI-PRE, like when everything gets scanned and then rolled back in slo-mo for a second scan while you endure the walk of shame, i.e., the Deluxe Frisk—the one that comes with an optional private room which sounds all comfy like a spa...

Except it isn't.

"Just think of it as a deep tissue massage," I tell myself as rude fingers press and push. Thankfully, I'm not ticklish when scared.

Adding insult to injury, my shoes are confiscated ("But… I'm TSA pre…") and searched like the steel-toed combat boots they're not. I call them socially acceptable slippers (by Walmart standards).

After I failed the tests a second time, I was told the issue: traces of an explosive material called Tetryl were detected on my laptop.

OK, I admit to being technologically inept, but I'm pretty sure I'd remember making an explosive device. Oh wait—I do recall not long ago mixing vinegar with baking soda to make a wacky cake (my mom's depression-era recipe).

As flattered as I am by the inference that my little half-brain could come up with something more diabolical than peeing in my sister's shoe that one time, I'm getting progressively less confident in my ability to convince them, and John isn't helping. "Well, you've always been MY favorite spy…" He whispers, "…undercovers." I elbow him. All the buzzing and questioning are confusing my mind.

I'm not stupid. I've seen Bourne Identity. Is it possible I inadvertently built an explosive while making ham and cheese sandwiches for our flight?

I'm not sure what's worrying me more: being sent to Guantanamo or having my TSA PRE status revoked before even once experiencing my true destiny: The glory of floating through security, head high, hair fluttering on the breeze, WITH MY SHOES ON!

Suddenly, an agent, zipping up my pack, says, "Okay-you're clear to go."

My eyebrows say, "WHAT?!" He explains, and I hear, "Blahblahblah...some kinds of meds/antihistamine contain tetryl... blahblahblah...so you're all clear."

Aha! I'd taken one sinus pill the night before. I must've accidentally licked my laptop. Who knows?

Problem solved— for the agents, anyway. Our TSA Pre remains untested, but we make our 6:15 morning flight out of Ottawa.

This incident turns out to be an example of "God working in mysterious ways," as revealed at U.S. customs ten hours later.

Once again, at security, my backpack is culled from the multitudes for a search. The young agent, looking serious in his crisp white emblemed shirt, asks the usual, "Where are you going, what do you do for a living, and please recite the preamble to the Constitution of the United States." (OK, I made that part up.) He's staring at the scanner and stops talking as he removes a heavy, roundish, bubble-wrapped object. He turns it around, studying it.

I start twitching as I realize what he's got and wonder how it got there. I pray a silent, "Oh please-no..."

But there it is—God's mysterious ways: Former TSA agents had been so distracted by the trace elements on my laptop that they failed to see—as had I— the real contraband I carried.

He looked me in the face and asked, "What's in here?"

"Ummm...I didn't know...I forgot to remove...well...that's my sour dough starter..."

He stares at me. I go on:

"I'm sorry—I...I meant to check it, but we left the house at 3:30 this morning and I guess I..."

He interrupts, "Oh—I see...how old is your starter, shouldn't you be keeping it cold?"

I'm struck dumb, recalibrating his intent. This agent is no threat—he's asking HOW OLD my starter is—a question only a seasoned baker would ask.

"Ummm," I stutter, "It travels well...very resilient... It's not my oldest... I made it upon arrival to Canada 19 months ago..."

He nods interest, "Yeah— I see."

A brief second —or eternity—goes by as he writes something. Then He smiles, hands me my jar of liquid gold, and says,

"Welcome Home."

Now we live with this expectation...an inheritance that is kept in heaven for you...beyond the reach of change...
1 Peter 1:3,4

And now, Lord, for what do I wait?
My hope is in You.
Psalm 39:7

The Lord of hosts has sworn: "As I have planned, so shall it be, and as I have purposed, so shall it stand."
Isaiah 14:24 ESV

> ### Sourdough Bread
>
> Mix:
> 1 cup starter
> 5 cups flour
> 1 pkg yeast
> 21/2 teas. salt
> 1-1/2 c water.
> Knead 8-10 min. Cover and rest 90 min. Shape into two loaves. Make cuts on the top of each loaf. Dust with flour, Let rise until double 1 hour. Bake 425° 30 minutes.
>
> Serve to TSA agents.

Made in the USA
Middletown, DE
23 October 2023

41164956R00139